RETHINKING HUMAN RIGHTS AND GLOBAL CONSTITUTIONALISM: FROM INCLUSION TO BELONGING

Are human rights really a building block of global constitutionalism? Does global constitutionalism have any future in the theory and practice of international law and global governance? This book critically examines these key questions by focusing on the mechanisms utilised by global constitutionalism while comparing the historical functioning of constitutional rights in national systems. Yahyaoui Krivenko provides new insights into the workings of human rights and associated notions, such as the state, the political, and the individual, by demonstrating that human rights are antithetical to global constitutionalism and encouraging new discussions on the meaning of global constitutionalism and human rights. Drawing on the interdisciplinary works of such thinkers as Agamben, Luhmann, Bourdieu, Deleuze and Guattari, this book also considers practical examples from historical experience of ancient Greek and early Islamic societies. It will appeal to scholars interested in human rights, international law and critical legal theory.

EKATERINA YAHYAOUI KRIVENKO is a lecturer at the Irish Centre for Human Rights, School of Law, National University of Ireland Galway, with expertise in gender, migration, and theoretical approaches to global ordering. In 2016 she received NUI Galway President's award for research excellence. She acted as an independent expert for the EU Horizon2020 Programme.

RETHINKING HUMAN RIGHTS AND GLOBAL CONSTITUTIONALISM

From Inclusion to Belonging

EKATERINA YAHYAOUI KRIVENKO

CAMBRIDGE
UNIVERSITY PRESS

CAMBRIDGE
UNIVERSITY PRESS

University Printing House, Cambridge CB2 8BS, United Kingdom

One Liberty Plaza, 20th Floor, New York, NY 10006, USA

477 Williamstown Road, Port Melbourne, VIC 3207, Australia

4843/24, 2nd Floor, Ansari Road, Daryaganj, Delhi – 110002, India

79 Anson Road, #06–04/06, Singapore 079906

Cambridge University Press is part of the University of Cambridge.

It furthers the University's mission by disseminating knowledge in the pursuit of education, learning, and research at the highest international levels of excellence.

www.cambridge.org
Information on this title: www.cambridge.org/9781107122024
DOI: 10.1017/9781316387931

First published 2017

Printed in the United Kingdom by Clays, St Ives plc

A catalogue record for this publication is available from the British Library.

Library of Congress Cataloging-in-Publication Data
Names: Yahyaoui Krivenko, Ekaterina, author.
Title: Rethinking human rights and global constitutionalism : from inclusion to belonging / Ekaterina Yahyaoui Krivenko.
Description: New York, NY : Cambridge University Press, 2017. | Includes bibliographical references and index.
Identifiers: LCCN 2017025812 | ISBN 9781107122024 (hardback)
Subjects: LCSH: Human rights. | Civil rights. | Constitutional law – Philosophy. | BISAC: LAW / International.
Classification: LCC K3240 .Y333 2017 | DDC 341.4/8–dc23
LC record available at https://lccn.loc.gov/2017025812

ISBN 978-1-107-12202-4 Hardback

To my husband, Yahyaoui M.B.S., my constant supporter and companion. I learned from him the foundations of thought in audacity, but with calm.

CONTENTS

ACKNOWLEDGEMENTS

The research leading to this book was supported by a grant from the People Programme (Marie Curie Actions) of the European Union's Seventh Framework Programme (FP7/2007–2013) under REA grant agreement PCIG13-GA-2013-618183. Some of the ideas examined in this book were presented and discussed at different conferences and workshops. My gratitude goes towards all who through their interest, comments and criticism encouraged further work on this book.

My special gratitude goes to the staff of the Max Planck Institute for Comparative Public Law and International Law in Heidelberg, in particular to Professor Anne Peters. This place provided an ideal environment for focused academic work in the last months of writing.

Introduction

A Context and Plan of Work

Constitutionalism understood broadly is a concept that addresses emergence, restriction and legitimation of power and authority. Traditionally, concepts of constitutions and constitutionalism developed from within particular communities, mostly states. In this sense, international or global constitutionalism[1] implies a qualitative shift in thinking: how to apply constitutional concepts beyond nation-states and bounded communities. Global constitutionalism as a way of reflecting upon authority and power at the global level proliferated with the intensification of processes subsumed under the heading of globalisation.

Global constitutionalism is a popular subject within the field of public international law,[2] although many international law scholars adopt a rather sceptical attitude towards the idea of global constitutionalism.[3] The basic idea behind the modern international constitutionalist movement is the necessity to introduce better control over the exercise of power at the global level. Human rights form a core of the global constitutionalist project. Imitating modern nation-state constitutions emanating from Western legal and political tradition, which views constitutional rights as guarantees against state interference with individual freedoms,

[1] The choice and the use of the terms 'international constitutionalism' or 'global constitutionalism' will be explained and justified at the beginning of Chapter 1.

[2] For some recent examples, in chronological order, see Dunoff and Trachtman (eds.) *Ruling the World* (2009); Klabbers, Peters and Ulfstein, *Constitutionalization* (2009); Kleinlein, *Konstitutionalisierung* (2011); Schwöbel, *Global Constitutionalism* (2011); Krisch, *Beyond Constitutionalism* (2012); Teubner, *Constitutional Fragments* (2012); Habermas, 'Crisis' (2012); Somek, *Cosmopolitan Constitution* (2014); Kjaer, *Constitutionalism* (2014); O'Donoghue, *Constitutionalism* (2014); Bhandari, *Global Constitutionalism* (2016).

[3] For an overview of skeptics see d'Aspremont, 'International Legal Constitutionalism' or Werner, 'Never-Ending Closure'.

various theories of international constitutionalism postulate human rights as limits on and protections against the arbitrary use of power by states and other global actors. However, the relationship between human rights and the project of international constitutionalism is articulated in the doctrine of public international law only rudimentarily. When human rights are discussed as a part of theories of international constitutionalism, the discussions are very brief and based on generalisations. The majority of the existing discussions are grounded in the following two fundamental assumptions:

- Global constitutionalism can only be developed by mimicking national constitutional orders of Western nation-states;[4]
- International human rights law forms an unchallengeable basis for the project of global constitutionalism.[5]

These assumptions emerge from an uncritical belief in the undisputable positive nature and effect of human rights as well as the presumption in favour of the Western constitutional experience. The absence of an alternative language and imagery able to address the need for limiting the exercise of power at the global level is also a serious obstacle. While some alternatives to the idea of global constitutionalism as a device for reflecting upon ordering and power constraints at the global level have emerged – such as, for example, the literature on transnational or global pluralism or global administrative law – they also rely to a greater or smaller extent on human rights without examining the underlying assumptions behind this reliance.

The present study takes a critical view on the issue of global constitutionalism and its relationship to the international protection of human rights. The place attributed to human rights within global constitutionalism is particularly important for several reasons. The introduction of

[4] See e.g. the discussion of constitutional features of international human rights in Gardbaum, 'Human Rights', 238. For a more explicit example, see Paulus' contribution to the same volume where he evaluates the 'progress and potential of constitutionalisation in general international law ... using established principles of domestic constitutions'. Paulus, 'International Legal System', 90.

[5] This is a general idea that follows from the almost complete absence of any consideration by the theories of global constitutionalism of the existing literature taking a critical stand with regard to the international system of human rights protection. Even if the existence of this critical literature is acknowledged, the usefulness and use of human rights is maintained in the absence of any substitute. An exemplary statement would be 'Who could deny the worldwide validity, higher right, and constitutional rank of universal human rights?' Teubner, *Constitutional Fragments*, 124.

human rights into the constitutional structures of nation-states and now of the international community is said to form a cornerstone of effective protection of individuals against the arbitrary use of power. However, if the human rights promise of protection is just an illusion, the danger of abuses and misuse is real and significant. Moreover, power-holders will be able to excuse their abuses by reference to the supposedly constitutional structure that integrates human rights protection. In order to prevent human rights from becoming a more authoritative legitimating device in the hands of power-holders, there is an urgent need to understand how human rights function within the project of constitutionalisation in international law. There is also a need to find an alternative language and imagery for the desire that drives international lawyers towards the production of constitutional theories. While many share idealistic aspirations of global constitutionalism, such as promoting individual well-being and imposing constraints on power exercised by global actors, the implications and consequences of the uncritical use of constitutionalist language relying on human rights can be problematic.

The idea of human rights forming one of the central building blocks of theories of global constitutionalism has itself been subjected to strong critical analysis by some scholars.[6] Therefore, this study pursues two interrelated aims: (1) to examine how human rights function within the emerging global (possibly constitutional) order and reassess their role at the global level (explored in Chapters 1 and 2); and (2) to suggest strategies for developing an alternative imagery that is able to respond to global constitutionalism's idealistic aspirations while avoiding conventional traps (explored in Chapters 3 and 4). In achieving its aims, the study argues that dominant paradigms of global constitutionalism are based on an exclusion/inclusion dynamic that always necessarily leads to some degree of arbitrariness and injustice. Therefore, the study argues for a rethinking of dominant paradigms of global constitutionalism. With regard to human rights, the main argument is that human rights do not function as constraints on the arbitrary exercise of power and protections of individuals in the way assumed in global constitutionalist discourse. To the contrary, they represent one of the central mechanisms maintaining the exclusion/inclusion dynamic with its injustices. Therefore, there is a need for alternative mechanisms of power-constraint and individual protection. In order to overcome the dominant paradigms of global constitutionalism these alternative mechanisms need to be searched for in non-Western,

[6] See e.g. Chandler, *Rethinking*; Douzinas, *Human Rights*; Kennedy, *Dark Sides*.

non-state-centred contexts. This study proposes alternatives based on analyses of ancient Greece and early Islam. As a result of these analyses, the proposed alternative vision of global constitutionalism focuses on the broad aim of enabling a happy life together and suggests strategies to move away from exclusion/inclusion logic towards the idea of belonging.

In order to achieve the objectives and develop a persuasive argument, an interdisciplinary approach, understood here as the use of methodologies and insights from disciplines other than law for the analysis of legal issues, appeared indispensable. The interdisciplinary methodology adopted in this study is twofold. On the one hand, methodologies and insights from other disciplines oriented the general approach of this study: the way questions are asked, the structure and the way of looking for alternatives. The core of this interdisciplinary element is constituted by the methodological approaches derived from the works of Giorgio Agamben[7] and Gilles Deleuze and Félix Guattari.[8] Therefore, before proceeding towards the analysis of substantive issues, the next part of this introduction clarifies these methodological approaches and some of their central tools. On the other hand, when discussing specific issues in order to gain deeper insights into particular sub-areas, analyses from other disciplines, mostly sociology, became indispensable. These alternative interdisciplinary insights are justified and clarified in the relevant parts of this study.

The substantive discussion of this study starts with a general overview of the place of constitutionalism in public international law. In this first chapter some definitions of basic concepts are provided, followed by a critical review of the scholarly views on the issue of global constitutionalism using paradigmatic and functional analysis. In order to identify relevant paradigms within the doctrine of global constitutionalism, existing theories are approached with three main questions in mind: What role do individuals play within the proposed system? What meaning and place is attributed to states and sovereignty? What is the nature of the political that various constitutionalisms presuppose? The examination of these questions will assist in getting a better understanding of how precisely human rights function within particular theories of global constitutionalism, a question that will be examined in Chapter 2. Overall, Chapter 1 concludes that all paradigms of global

[7] The main reference in this regard is Agamben, *Signature*.

[8] The work of these authors that forms the basis for the methodological reflections in this study is Deleuze and Guattari, *Kafka*.

constitutionalism are based on an exclusion/inclusion dynamic that necessarily leaves some groups of human beings out of the realm of protection, and thus produces arbitrariness and injustice. For each paradigm the chapter also offers a reflection on possible ways of overcoming the exclusion/inclusion dynamic.

Chapter 2 takes a critical view of the functioning of human rights. Since the main question that the chapter examines is how human rights function, the use of a sociological system theory appeared to be the most appropriate tool. After examining and comparing the historical functioning of constitutional rights in national constitutional systems and the functioning of human rights at the international level, the chapter comes to the following conclusions. First, it is still difficult to draw a clear picture of the functioning of international human rights. However, in the present state of knowledge about the functioning of human rights, we can affirm with certainty that human rights do not function similarly to constitutional rights in domestic settings. More significantly, while human rights do occasionally protect individuals against abuses of power, this is not their main goal. The main mechanism human rights activate is the exclusion/inclusion mechanism identified as common to all paradigms, which were covered in Chapter 1. Therefore, relying on human rights to constrain arbitrary exercise of power will necessarily produce arbitrary results. The chapter concludes that there is an urgent need for alternative mechanisms for power constraints and individual protections at the global level.

Chapter 3 explores these alternative accounts of power control. Since the initial criticism of current theories of global constitutionalism that gave impetus to this research mainly focuses on the predominance of Western constitutional experience (Eurocentrism) and the unquestioned acceptance of rights language (rights-oriented nature), I selected one non-Western normative order (Islam) and one non-legal normative order (ancient Greece) to examine some alternative strategies for power control. These alternative strategies combined with suggestions about overcoming the exclusion/inclusion dynamic formulated in relation to paradigms of global constitutionalism point towards the idea of belonging as the guiding tool for reorienting global ordering. The Chapter 4 represents a summary of the analysis and further reflections articulating how the project of global constitutionalism as a happy life together could potentially become part of the reoriented idea of global ordering as belonging.

B On Methodology

The approach adopted in this study emerged out of a strongly felt need for a deep and multifaceted understanding of the issues involved and the conviction that such an understanding could only materialise through the application of a methodology allowing for the approach of issues from a new angle. At the same time, it was necessary that this new angle have the potential of leading the study into the direction determined by its objectives without predetermining outcomes and conclusions: that is, to examine how human rights function as parts of the theories of global constitutionalism and open up a new language and imagery for dealing with issues that lead international law scholars into the direction of global constitutionalism. In order to achieve these objectives, it was important to find an appropriate perspective that could guide the reflection on these issues, a sort of a meta-method that guides the thinking process and orients the way questions are asked without necessarily re-emerging in the discussion of substantive issues. This section clarifies this meta-method.

The first important preoccupation relates to the almost complete absence of an in-depth discussion of the mechanism of human rights within the existing theories of global constitutionalism. The dominant literature rather proceeds from an untested and unquestioned assumption that human rights with their current functions will become or are already part of global constitutionalism. For some authors the very existence and functioning of human rights in their present form in international law becomes proof of existence of the constitutionalised international society. In order to interrogate this problem anew, Deleuze and Guattari's literary analysis method of looking at how a particular theme functions within an author's oeuvre provided an inspiration.

The phenomenon of global constitutionalism, and its links to human rights, is a modern, contemporary development. However, it has a history, albeit perhaps not a very long one compared to some other problems of humanity. Simultaneously, one of the main objectives in undertaking this study was also to project the ideas developing around human rights and constitutionalisation of international law into the future, proposing innovative visions and language. Thus, present, past and future needed to come together in a non-linear way to reveal new insights. Giorgio Agamben's depiction of philosophical archaeology as a future anterior that gains access to the present for the first time[9] provided an ideal framework in this regard.

9 Agamben, *Signature*, 106.

In what follows, I present my understanding of these two approaches: Agamben's philosophical archaeology and Deleuze and Guattari's method of literary analysis, and I justify in more detail their influence on and usefulness for the present study.

1 *Agamben and Philosophical Archaeology*

The three essays on method published within a single volume entitled *The Signature of All Things: On Method* deal with different but interrelated issues of paradigm, signature and philosophical archaeology. The essay on philosophical archaeology is placed as the third and final of the three essays. The most interesting characteristic of philosophical archaeology is its relationship to time. As the term 'archaeology' indicates, it deals with the past and the origin (*archē*). However, the relationship to the past and access to the past is of a particular nature. The origin is also understood in a particular way. Summarising the aim of philosophical archaeology, Agamben states, 'the point of archaeology is to gain access to the present for the first time, beyond memory and forgetting or, rather, at the threshold of their indifference.'[10] The access to the present is gained for the first time because the 'origin' that is at stake is not some temporarily locatable moment in the past, but 'a moment of arising' that was 'covered over and neutralized by tradition'.[11] This neutralisation is compared to repression in psychoanalysis so that what was repressed becomes unconscious and haunts the present.[12] However, unlike in psychoanalysis, the goal is not 'to restore a previous stage, but to decompose, displace, and ultimately, bypass it in order to go back *not to its content, but to the modalities, circumstances*, and moments in which the split, by means of repression, constituted it as origin'.[13] It will become clear that this emphasis on modalities and circumstances as opposed to content is an important aspect that unites philosophical archaeology with Deleuze and Guattari's approach. It should also be noted that this access to the modalities in which the split occurred is particularly relevant for Chapter 2, where the suppressed exclusion/inclusion dynamic of human rights is revealed.

Agamben emphasises the necessity to engage anew sources and tradition that is only possible if the tradition is confronted through deconstruction of 'the *paradigms, techniques, and practices* through which tradition regulates the forms of transmission, conditions access to

[10] Ibid. [11] Ibid., 105. [12] Ibid., 96–98, 102–103. [13] Ibid., 103, emphasis added.

sources, and in the final analysis determines *the very status of the knowing subject*'.[14] Three aspects of this statement need to be highlighted. Firstly, the importance of paradigms as building blocks on the way towards achieving the aim of philosophical archaeology is emphasised. This explains why the first chapter of the study is dedicated to identifying relevant paradigms within the theories of constitutionalisation of international law. Secondly, the statement places paradigms at the same level of importance as technics and practices. Deleuze and Guattari propose one methodology that is particularly useful in identifying and understanding any aspect related to the functioning of a particular phenomenon, including techniques and practices. Therefore, Agamben's method of philosophical archaeology is combined with Deleuze and Guattari's method, which will be addressed below.

One final observation on philosophical archaeology is necessary. It creates a very peculiar relationship between the past, the present and the future that serves well the purposes of this study. It simultaneously allows us to gain access to the present through a deeper engagement with the past, but also to imagine the future because the space opening up in the past is projected into the future.

2 *Deleuze and Guattari: Machinic Assemblage and How It Functions*

The second methodological approach is inspired by one specific work of Deleuze and Guattari, their book *Kafka: Towards a Minor Literature*. In this book they approach the works of Kafka as a minor literature and provide their interpretation of how Kafka's oeuvre functions as such. The notion of minor literature itself is not central to our purposes. Therefore, I will just briefly define it in order to facilitate the subsequent discussion of Deleuze and Guattari's approach.[15] The methodological tools that I borrow from this book are developed by Deleuze and Guattari in order to explain *how* Kafka's oeuvre *functions* as a minor literature.

According to Deleuze and Guattari the following are the three characteristics of a minor literature: 'the language is affected by high coefficient of deterritorialisation'; 'everything in them is political'; and 'in it everything takes on a collective value'.[16] They argue that Kafka was an

[14] Ibid., 89, emphasis added.

[15] For a more detailed discussion of the notion of minor literature and reading international law as a minor literature see Yahyaoui Krivenko, 'International Law'.

[16] Deleuze and Guattari, *Kafka*, 16–17.

author of a minor literature and they want to understand the mechanisms that allow Kafka to operate as an author of minor literature. In order to achieve this, Deleuze and Guattari adopt a particular approach that influenced this study.

Deleuze and Guattari proceed from a few fundamental principles that need to be highlighted from the outset. Firstly, they refuse a search for a structure with formal binary oppositions.[17] Instead, they use their terminology of machinery, machines and assemblages that emphasises the interconnectedness of everything and the equal importance of every single element, movement, gesture. This also implies an absence of distinction between inside and outside, and emphasis on process rather than form. Thus, they refuse the search for some hidden and fundamental meaning, focusing instead on understanding functioning, the way a particular theme or image works within the author's oeuvre. In this sense, traditional literary interpretation in their case and traditional doctrinal approach of international law in the case of this study become useless. This emphasis on functioning and mechanisms has several affinities with Agamben's depiction of philosophical archaeology. When Agamben says that the movement towards the past of philosophical archaeology is not towards its content, but towards its modalities and circumstances,[18] it resonates with the following observation by Deleuze and Guattari that summarises well the essence of their approach: 'It is absolutely useless to look for a theme in a writer if one hasn't asked exactly what its importance is in the work – that is, how it functions (and not what its "sense" is).'[19] In order to understand this functioning of Kafka's oeuvre, Deleuze and Guattari adopt a particular perspective and terminology. Running the danger of simplification but keeping in mind the need for brevity, I describe below the elements essential for my further discussion and for understanding the approach of the present study.

Kafka's oeuvre is described as a machinic assemblage. In order to understand how this assemblage functions, we also need to identify its building blocks, its elements and how they are connected to each other. The assemblage commences to be built through creation of machinic indexes that will become parts of the assemblage. This assemblage being built seems to indicate some mysterious function. The best example of such machinic indexes is provided by Kafka's animalistic stories that can be read as complete finished works conveying some hidden meaning.

[17] Ibid., 7. [18] See note 13 above and the accompanying text.
[19] Deleuze and Guattari, *Kafka*, 45.

However, if we realise that these indexes are only parts or signs of an assemblage – and thinking of Kafka's writings as single oeuvre helps in achieving this realisation – we can at some point understand how these parts fit together and what type of assemblage they compose. The assemblage at work becomes visible in novels. However, Deleuze and Guattari distinguish assemblages from abstract machines that are also sort of finished assemblages but don't function or no longer function.[20] The assemblages themselves can function in two ways: they can be in the process of being assembled or they can work towards their own dismantling: 'Writing has a double function: to translate everything into assemblages and to dismantle the assemblages. The two are the same thing.'[21] Therefore, there is an intimate link between abstract machines and machinic assemblages. Abstract machines can help evaluate degree and mode of assemblages: to what extent assemblages are real, in the sense of their capacity to dismantle themselves, and not mere abstract machines. (Transcendental law and immanent field of justice can be given as examples of abstract machine and machinic assemblage, respectively.) Chapter 1 focuses on identifying paradigms of global constitutionalism as building blocks or indexes in Deleuze and Guattari's terminology, while Chapter 2 depicts human rights as a particular type of mechanism.

This brief discussion of the Deleuze and Guattari's approach to minor literature and their way of looking at how this functions within the oeuvre of Kafka served to introduce the basic methodological background that is used to attempt a renewed look at the issue of constitutionalisation of international law and its relationship to human rights. Against the background of this discussion by Deleuze and Guattari it became obvious that the fundamental question this study needs to address is *how* human rights function within the oeuvre of public international law, not what function they fulfil or what meaning they have.

One final point that needs justification is the transposition of this method from the analysis of the works produced by one single author to the body of literature emanating from a variety of authors. Since international lawyers produce written work, they also produce an oeuvre, although it is not a literary oeuvre in the traditional sense. We can approach as a single oeuvre, not only writings of a particular international law scholar, but also writings constituting international law as such. International law abides by quite strict rules that determine its disciplinary boundaries, accepted styles, themes, etc. This produces a

[20] Ibid., 47. [21] Ibid.

certain unity that can be analysed as a connected whole. Therefore, at least as a meta-methodology in the sense explained above, Deleuze and Guattari's insights can be extended to the area under investigation here.

3 *Building Blocks, Paradigms: Time-Travel Machines?*

The above brief overview of the two methodological approaches guiding this study demonstrates a series of affinities between them. Both place emphasis on processes and techniques, rather than meanings. At first sight, the difference between approaches might appear to emerge from their relationship to time. One being more concerned with the past, the other with the present. This distinction is true only as a matter of degree or emphasis. Agamben's philosophical archaeology is as much if not more concerned with the present or more specifically with understanding the ways in which the past determines the present, and thus opening up a possibility of projection into the future. Deleuze and Guattari are focusing on machines, their parts, connectors and how they function. If we consider that a functioning of a machine is a continuing process – they often talk about assemblages in the process of being assembled and then being dismantled – then their approach is also equally concerned with the past, the present and the future. They simply focus on mechanics more than on the timeline itself. But is not understanding mechanics of a phenomenon the best way of being able to influence this phenomenon – either by interrupting, accelerating or modifying it? And is not the possibility of being able to intervene into the functioning of a particular machine the best way to influence the future? In this sense both approaches complement each other. Together, they provide a methodological tool able to serve the purposes of the present study: to understand how human rights function as a part of the project of constitutionalisation of international law and to formulate some strategies for the future based on this deeper understanding.

1

Paradigms of Global Constitutionalism

The aim of this chapter is to depict existing theories of global constitutionalism by identifying their foundational paradigms. The focus will not be on the opinions of particular authors, but on recurrent crosscutting issues that determine the way any discussion on global constitutionalism is framed and how particular themes function within it. However, in order to identify these crosscutting issues and themes, it will be necessary to analyse positions of different authors. In order to better situate different theories, a brief initial overview of the broad framework of global constitutionalism and related issues is provided.

A Situating Global Constitutionalism

Constitutionalism is a way of constituting something, 'constitute' meaning to 'establish', 'create'. In its Latin form *'constituere'* means 'set up', 'fix', 'form something new'. This in turn derives from *'stāre'*: 'to stand firmly without moving'.[1] The same root is at the origin of the word 'state'.[2] The link between the state and the idea of constitutionalism is not only theoretically or historically constructed, but exists at a deeper linguistic level.

Constitutionalism can have at least two meanings in relation to a state. The first meaning is very close to the ordinary meaning of the word 'constitute' from which it derives: to establish, to create a state. It can best be expressed in the following way: 'By constitution we mean . . . that assemblage of laws, institutions and customs . . . that compose the general system, according to which the community hath agreed to be governed.'[3] The second meaning is more specific and refers to the

[1] Rolland, *Familles*. This in turn goes back to the Indo-European root *stā-*, meaning 'to stand'. See e.g. Pokorny, *Wörterbuch*, vol. 3, 1004–1008.

[2] Rolland, *Familles*. [3] Bolingbroke, *Dissertation*, 108.

restrictions placed on the ruling power, on the government: 'All constitutional government is by definition limited government.'[4] For the purposes of the present study, this later meaning of constitutionalism is of much greater significance because protection of individuals' rights acquires prominence with the growth of this second, more specific meaning of constitutionalism. This distinction between two meanings of constitutionalism retains its usefulness as an analytical tool despite its slightly artificial character. While employing it as an analytical tool, the present study places greater emphasis on the simultaneity of these two meanings of constitutionalism. Every society that is in the process of structuring itself (the first meaning of constitutionalism) is also at the same time limiting the power it creates (the second meaning of constitutionalism). Simply, in our modern understanding of constitutionalism in the second sense, we usually require certain more advanced and pronounced limits on the exercise of power, perhaps even limits in some predefined forms, such as separation of powers or human rights.

Thus, the basic idea behind contemporary theories of constitutionalism can be described as an imposition of constraints on power. However, more broadly, constitutionalism can be said to deal with authority and the exercise of power from their production to their restraint and legitimation. When trying to formulate the fundamental question that modern constitutionalism addresses, contemporary scholars focus on the centrality of the individual and his/her freedom: 'In all cases, constitutionalism serves as a reminder of modernity's resilient ambition for the collective self constitution of the social and political world in a moral universe in which the individual is the basic unit.'[5] However, this focus on the autonomous individual and his freedom conceived in a negative fashion (freedom from something), inspired by Enlightenment, is definitely a later addition to constitutionalism.

When reflecting on the broad meaning of constitutionalism as addressing power and authority from their production to restraint and legitimation, we can logically extend this type of thinking beyond states. In

[4] McIlwain, *Constitutionalism*, 21. A similar distinction can be found in Wormuth, *Origins*, 1.

[5] Walker, 'Constitutionalism and Pluralism', 27. The same idea is expressed by Dippel when formulating the central question of constitutionalism: 'How individual liberty could be made permanently secure against encroachments of the government and with regard to the weaknesses of human nature' (Dippel, 'Modern Constitutionalism', 154). Similarly, ButleRitchie, 'Confines'; or Castiglione, 'Political Theory'.

this broad sense constitutional questions have been debated and addressed wherever there was some form of basic organisation of social interaction. We should be cautious when using the term 'constitutionalism' to designate these broader efforts of structuring communities in a way leading to their prosperity that took place outside modern European tradition because the term itself is so heavily ideologically loaded. However, it is important for the purposes of this book to situate constitutionalism as a part of a broader tradition directed at securing the well-being of communities and their members. This will open up the possibilities for an exploration of ideas outside of the modern European tradition in subsequent chapters. Nevertheless, even if we extend constitutional thinking in a broad sense beyond the Western concept of the state, we have to admit that these efforts at organising human life and thus forming communities were traditionally directed at delimited (although not always very precisely) groups of human beings, such as Greek city-states, particular religious communities, medieval cities or later nation-states, to give just a few examples. It is only with the development of what can be called modernity that scholars started discussing systematically the possibility and modalities of extending constitutionalism and its interrogations to the whole of humanity, to the entirety of the globe.[6]

Developments described under the heading of globalisation prompted a growth of literature on several issues related to constitutionalism as applied to the global realm. This literature, utilising different approaches, is generated from a variety of disciplinary perspectives. The present study focuses on the literature produced from within the discipline of international law. Obviously, it is not always possible and desirable to draw strict disciplinary boundaries. Moreover, many scholars adopt truly inter- and multidisciplinary approaches. Nevertheless, there exists a clearly discernable core literature that self-identifies as representing the discipline of public international law, even if inspired by methods and approaches from other disciplines. The focus on this literature is dictated by the focus of the present study: the relationship between human rights and constitutionalism as applied to the whole globe. Human rights

[6] Obviously, some cosmopolitan ideals can be traced as far back as ancient Greek thought and other more ancient systems of thought. However, the question about the extent to which these cosmopolitan ideals prefigure international constitutionalist thinking is quite complex and requires further elaboration. It will be addressed to the extent required for the purposes of this study in Chapter 3.

raise a series of issues related to justice, protection, enforcement, and so on that tie them to public international law. In the language of human rights, states continue to appear as main guarantors of human rights despite the growth of literature addressing the responsibility of non-state actors for human rights violations. In addition, even in the discussion of roles and responsibilities of non-state actors in the field of human rights, the mediating role of states, states as a prism through which to approach non-state actors remain so far predominant.[7] Also, the traditionally existing link between states, on the one hand, and legal regulations and constitutions, on the other, still dominates the imagination of the majority of lawyers and non-lawyers alike despite recent examinations of regulations, regulatory networks and constitutional arrangements beyond states. The focus on global constitutionalism as addressed by the discipline of *international* law is not to deny the existence and importance of developments going beyond the state but to investigate how a discipline that is traditionally constructed around the idea of the state deals with all these developments while attempting to conserve its place as a distinctly legal field of study embracing the whole of humanity. On the other hand this study also argues that the existing attempts at going beyond the state are still only partially successful and have not yet overcome state thinking,[8] therefore the term *international* constitutionalism is justified when discussing the contemporary state of scholarship in international law. On the other hand, it will become clear that according to the position defended in this study, constitutionalism, if it has any future, can only be conceived as *global* constitutionalism, overcoming the divisions in states and nations. Therefore, depending on the emphasis, both terms – global and international constitutionalism – are employed.

Since clarifications and explanations of constitutional theories have been historically developed in relation to states and their internal structure, the most complete descriptions and discussions of constitutionalism will be found in relation to domestic constitutional theories. The importance of both the historical development of national constitutionalism as well as of the theories developed with

[7] This again is not to deny that efforts are made to think about the responsibility of non-state actors for human rights violations independently of states. However, the present author agrees with those diagnoses that highlight the continuing predominance of the state prism. See e.g. Teubner, *Constitutional Fragments*, Chapter 5.

[8] This argument is developed in the section 'States in Global Constitutionalism' in this chapter.

reference to domestic constitutions is further highlighted by the frequent reference to these domestic developments by international lawyers writing on international constitutionalism. In order to distinguish the theories developed and explanations provided with regard to constitutions and constitutional structures of nation-states from those relating to the international community and international law, the term internal or domestic constitutionalism is used to refer to the former and the expression international or global constitutionalism refers to the latter.

If we accept the correctness of the modern meaning of constitutionalism, we also accept the underlying presumption that a state, or any other type of structure that we attempt to constitutionalise, where government is unrestricted is not a complete or perfect state/structure. On the other hand, it should be kept in mind that in any process of establishment and creation constitutionalism can only be realised gradually, step by step. Hence, the use of term 'constitutionalisation'. Therefore, it can happen that despite some restrictions in place on the power of (a) ruler(s), there is still no perfect or achieved construction in place; the constitutionalism is still in process of being constituted. In the current state of the art, with regard to constitutionalism, there is no set of definitive and clear criteria that allow any form of constitutionalism to be regarded as a perfect or full achievement. Perhaps there will never be any definitive criteria of a perfect constitionalised society, and perhaps there never should be such an ideal finished product. However, it is important to be aware of the uncertainty surrounding the issue of constitutionalisation and the dialectics of duality between the broader and the narrower meanings of constitutionalism.

Thus, it appears from this summary analysis of the meaning of the term 'constitutionalism' that both visions of constitutionalism – the minimalist view of it as a way of establishing a community and the maximalist regard of it as a way of constraining the government's exercise of power – are, in reality, interwoven and situated within a continuum in which they are just two points. With regard to international or global constitutionalism, it is not yet clear where on this continuum that international constitutionalism in its current form is situated. Despite a wealth of literature on the notion of international community,[9] it remains debatable who, precisely, constitutes this international community that is now apparently in the process of being

[9] See e.g. Simma and Paulus, 'International Community'; and Karakulian, 'Idea', for a general overview with further references.

constitutionalised further:[10] who is the active subject of global constitutionalism and who is being empowered. Therefore, the following part of this chapter targets, among others, the precise contours of the international community as it emerges from the literature on international constitutionalism, focusing on two potential candidates for an active subject: individuals and states. Human rights bring individuals and states into a dialectical relationship that needs to be examined in detail if we want to understand precisely how international constitutionalism integrates human rights within its project. Therefore, two parts of this chapter are devoted to examining the dominant paradigms of international constitutionalism in relation to individuals and states.

Constitutions as documents and constitutionalism as a phenomenon are traditionally situated within the borders of a particular nation-state and presuppose a bounded community. Therefore, thinking about *international* or *global* constitutionalism implies a qualitative shift in the understanding of constitutionalism away from bounded community to diversity and away from a single territorial unit to an assemblage of a variety of such units. International lawyers writing about international constitutionalism do not always consciously reflect upon these shifts.[11] Many are tempted by a presupposition that the international community is bounded enough and our globe is an adequate territorial unit. Assuming this statement holds true, international lawyers cannot deny that the currently available international institutional and political structures significantly limit possibilities of interaction and meaningful political participation for several members of international community, but especially for individuals. Other scholars, acknowledging the diversity of the international community, develop ideas on how to achieve the required degree of unity comparable to domestic constitutionalist structures and communities. However, perhaps the qualitative difference of the 'international' or 'global' interactions resides precisely in their diversity and ability to embrace this diversity. This aspect is not sufficiently theorised in the literature on international constitutionalism and will be developed further through this study. In this chapter, this aspect will be theorised within the context of the analysis of paradigms related to the state and to the political.

On the basis of these initial reflections and interrogations contained therein, the remainder of the chapter is devoted to the identification of

[10] For a more detailed discussion of this point see O'Donoghue, *Constitutionalism*, 59–76.
[11] Rosenfeld, 'Modern Constitutionalism', 497.

underlying paradigms of international constitutionalism. To the extent possible, it also suggests avenues for overcoming these traditional paradigms. In order to identify these underlying paradigms, the following three parts of this chapter each focus on one of the three questions formulated based on the above discussion of constitutionalism:

- What role do individuals play within the proposed system of global constitutionalism? ('Individuals within Global Constitutionalism')
- What meaning and place is attributed to states and their sovereignty? ('States in Global Constitutionalism')
- What political structures do different theories presuppose or articulate as legitimate? ('Politics of International Constitutionalism')

These questions allow for the identification of underlying paradigms and for gaining a better understanding of how the doctrine of international constitutionalism responds to these fundamental interrogations of constitutional theory. This understanding will then allow a deeper comprehension of the functioning of human rights in global constitutionalism that will be discussed in Chapter 2.

B Theories of Constitutionalism: Questions, Gaps, Issues

When one attempts to present various visions of international constitutionalism, one is faced with a wealth of literature and opinions that somehow overlap but still differ in several aspects. Therefore, the temptation comes to start classifying these different views even if very schematically. In fact, many of the authors writing about international constitutionalism propose from the outset one or another form of classification of constitutional theories pertaining to the international or global scale.[12] Although classifications can be helpful in approaching such a wide field as international constitutionalism, they also have the disadvantage of simplifying and diverting attention from some intricacies of arguments developed by a particular author. For example, if an author defended a particular argument that does not fit easily with the overall characterisation of a category into which he or she was classified, the subsequent discussion tends to forget and overlook this argument. In order to avoid this type of simplification and generalisation, the

[12] See e.g. Fassbender, 'The United Nations Charter', 538–551; Klabbers, Peters and Ulfstein, *Constitutionalization*, 25–31; Schwöbel, *Global Constitutionalism*, Chapter 1; Teubner, 'Societal Constitutionalism'; Van Mulligen, 'Global Constitutionalism', 279.

subsequent discussion of various constitutional theories in international law is organised not around any general classification of theories, but around the three topics mentioned above that are important to the understanding of the relationship between human rights and international constitutionalism.

1 Individuals within Global Constitutionalism

a) The State of the Art: The Individual as an Equilibrium Point

Any discussion of international constitutionalism necessarily touches upon the issue of the place of individuals in international law. Since international constitutionalism aims at defining, delimiting and legitimating the power that affects individuals in one way or another, it cannot avoid considering directly or indirectly the place attributed to individuals. The stance of many representatives of international constitutionalism when they consider the position of the individual within their proposed constitutionalised international systems is well expressed as follows: 'At the very least, if individuals are directly affected by international law and governance, there must be adequate mechanisms for protecting their human rights.'[13]

Traditionally, states are considered the main subjects of international law. Despite all of the changes arguably generated by globalisation, states remain 'the basic units of currency'[14] in public international law. Obviously, states as main subjects of international law today function differently and play roles different from the role ascribed to them a decade or a century ago. However, as far as the discipline of international law is concerned, it is too early to affirm the demise of its state-centred nature. This is perfectly illustrated by the below discussion of the place of individuals in various scholarly discussions of international constitutionalism and is further addressed in the next part of this chapter on states in global constitutionalism. Despite the centrality of states to the discipline of public international law, the place of the individual in international law has traditionally attracted attention of international lawyers. Several authors over time have provided powerful arguments in favour of a broad

[13] Cohen, 'Constitutionalism', 130.

[14] Crawford, *Brownlie's Principles*, 16. In a similar vein see Shaw, *Public International Law*, 1, explaining the difference between national and international law: 'the principal subjects of international law are nations-states, not individual citizens'.

recognition of an active position of individuals within the system of international law, either as a statement of fact or as a formulation of an ideal.[15]

Any version of international constitutionalism will usually acknowledge that a constitutionalist reading of international law implies a more active role for and more attention to individuals. For some authors it can be even the main achievement of the constitutionalist reading of international law: 'The constitutionalist approach offers a new foundation for the view that the ultimate international legal subjects are individuals. Constitutionalism postulates that natural persons are the ultimate unit of legal concern.'[16] Other versions of international constitutionalism can be less straightforward in this regard. Nevertheless, they still maintain the increased significance of individuals as opposed to non-constitutionalised versions of public international law. Moving from the limited role individuals play today in public international law to the projected constitutionalised community these authors affirm that within the restructured constitutionalised community 'individuals and State organs simultaneously function both within the national and post-national communities and legal orders.'[17] Very often, the authors oscillate in their analysis of the existing international order between 'ought' and 'is' of a fully recognised subjecthood of individuals. They affirm the existence of individuals as subjects of international law side by side with states within the current framework of international law. At the same time they insist that without the constitutionalisation of international law the absolute authority of states over private individuals, and as a consequence the erosion of their status as active subjects, is inevitable.[18]

What is the evidence of the present active position of individuals as subjects of international law? How can individuals become even more active and influential in the constitutionalised international community? The answer to the former question is usually more detailed than that to the later. For example, in Fassbender's study of the UN Charter as a constitution of international community, the question of the individual's place in a system where states are principal members of the community is

[15] The following representative examples in chronological order illustrate the interest over time: Spiropoulos, 'L'individu' (1929); Segal, *L'individu* (1932); Remec, *Position of the Individual*, (1960); Tornaritis, *Individual as a Subject* (1972); Clapham, 'Role of the Individual' (2010); Gaja, 'Position of Individuals' (2010); Parlett, *Individual* (2010); Peters, *Jenseits der Menschenrechte* (2014).

[16] Peters, 'Moving Towards Constitutionalization', 129.

[17] De Wet, 'International Constitutional Order', 75.

[18] Ibid., 55 and 76.

raised: 'States, and not peoples or individual human beings are prima facie the principal members of the community constituted by the Charter. Is that an argument against the constitutional character of the Charter?'[19] The answer proved is exemplary of the opinions of several authors writing on international constitutionalism:

> The international legal community is made up of all subjects of international law – sovereign states, states enjoying a limited international legal personality, intergovernmental organizations, peoples and minorities, belligerent parties, individuals, as well as special entities like the Holy See.[20]

However, just a few pages before, he also affirmed that there is 'ample evidence of the fact that the Charter has left behind the traditional state-centric view of international law, by gearing its rules to the ultimate goal of the general welfare of peoples and individual human beings'.[21] What is this evidence of the general welfare orientation of the UN Charter? How do these two statements relate to each other and what are implications of the fact that they are contained within a single version of global constitutionalism?

According to Fassbender, the UN Charter's mentioning of 'people' of the UN combined with its references to human rights protection demonstrates that behind states are people and behind people are individuals: the ultimate concern of any constitutionalised community.[22] Thus, the position of individuals in international law in this vision of international constitutionalism is necessarily mediated through states and people. This in turn implies that individuals who are not included in the active membership of either states or people will face significant difficulties having their voices and opinions heard at the international level. The most prominent examples of groups of human beings whose voices will be excluded under this scenario are refugees, asylum seekers, and several categories of migrants, including undocumented migrants. Theories of international constitutionalism do not tackle this issue.[23] There is rather

[19] Fassbender, *Charter as the Constitution*, 101. [20] Ibid., 134.

[21] Ibid., 102, also repeated in general conclusion of the chapter at 179. [22] Ibid., 102.

[23] Even outside the theories of global constitutionalism, the most recent contribution to the topic by Peters, a more than 500-page study defending the thesis that individuals become subjects of international law, devotes to refugee law only a few pages (400–406), concluding that 'Weil die Flüchtlingsrechte nicht selbst Menschenrechte sind, dürfen diese subjective-internationale Rechte durch Vertragsänderungen gekürzt oder augehoben werden, sofern nicht der menschenrechtliche Kern berührt wird.' Peters, *Jenseits der Menschenrechte*, 406. ['Since refugee rights are not themselves human rights, these

a constant swinging back and forth between an affirmation that a truly constitutionalised society (including at the international level) should have individuals as the primary unit of concern and a belief that the existence of human rights as a part of the corpus of international law is a sufficient proof of this concern and thus of a constitutional or at least constitutionalising nature of international law.

While the individual remains the centre to which everything returns, or using the image of a pendulum, the equilibrium point, human rights appear as the pivot or even the gravitational force that makes this constant return possible. Being the centre does not necessarily mean being active or having influence on its own fate. The centre can also be used in instrumental ways. Similarly, the protection and care a legal system affords to a particular issue, subject or thing does not necessarily mean the object of protection is an active subject whose opinions and views matter. It should be mentioned that Peters' recent book, which addresses the status of the individual in international law, attempts a refutation of this reading of the position of the individual in international law, suggesting a paradigm shift that makes individuals the *primary* international legal persons. For a series of reasons that can be detailed here only briefly, the present author disagrees with this diagnosis. Two of the most important elements in disagreement are the following. The above-mentioned mediation through states persists even in Peters' analysis. For example, in order to affirm the existence of the individuals as primary subjects of international law, Peters relies on the traditional sources of international law as listed in Art. 38 of the ICJ Statute[24] that are still shaped predominantly by states despite all the possibilities for individuals to influence formation of international law.[25] Peters herself expressly recognises the continuing predominance of states in several regards, most importantly implementation,[26] but continues nevertheless to insist on the *need* to have a foundation for individuals' status in international law independent of states.[27] The second reason follows from the first, particularly from the continuing dependence on states for implementation. This arguably emerging subjectivity of the individual remains highly selective. If individuals become primary subjects of international law at all, it is not

subjective international rights can be cancelled or restricted through a treaty modification as long as the human rights core is unaffected'. Author's translation.] This statement places refugees outside the general framework and opens a way to a wide state discretion. At the time of writing the English version of the book was not yet available, therefore, all references are to the German version.

[24] Ibid., 382. [25] Ibid., 474–479. [26] Ibid., 385. [27] Ibid.

just any individual, but only some privileged individuals. Therefore, as far as *practice* of contemporary *international law* is concerned, Hanna Arendt's discussion on 'a right to have rights' is as relevant as ever[28] because the right to have rights or more precisely, in the contemporary context, the right to enjoy a right and having an active status still largely depends on the state of residence or nationality of an individual.

In sum, using the existence of human rights protection and some additional rights enjoyed by individuals in other areas of international law as a proof of the central and active role of individuals in the constitutionalised international community is self-defeating as long as the functioning of human rights is not examined. It is important to understand whether and how human rights or other alternative mechanisms allow individuals to become the active and influential actors advocated by constitutionalism. Furthermore, by focusing exclusively on human rights or other legal developments in the field of international law as a way to achieve an active position for individuals in international law, proponents of international constitutionalism overlook another historically more important set of mechanisms that traditionally allowed active participation of individuals in making decisions affecting their own fate. This set of mechanisms is of a political nature. Such notions as democracy and constituent power are key terms that point towards this constitutionalist tradition. This set of mechanisms will be addressed in more detail in the final part of this chapter. At this stage, it is important to emphasise that a full articulation of the place of individuals in international law and global constitutionalism cannot be complete without considering both the legal and political mechanisms implicated.

As already mentioned, the dominant view is that individuals are or will become subjects of international law side by side with more traditional subjects, in particular states. According to my research, until today no scholar of international law has attempted to imagine a system of global constitutionalism that would exclude or disregard states. Depending on the position of a particular author, states are called to play a more or less active and influential role in their version of a constitutionalised international community, but no one has ever claimed that states will become completely irrelevant. Even the theories of societal constitutionalism or theories based on normative pluralism shifting clearly *beyond* the state do not actually propose a vision of constitutionalism or an alternative ordering *without* the state. Therefore, the next part of this chapter

[28] Arendt, *The Origins of Totalitarianism*, 290–302, especially 296–297.

examines in more detail what role exactly is reserved for states and their sovereignty in the constitutionalised international society. However, before considering the paradigm of the state within international constitutionalism, the next section of this part will attempt to better grasp mechanisms that are activated within a legal system when individuals can claim rights and influence decisions affecting them. This should allow us to better assess the available mechanisms at the level of international law, both here and in subsequent parts.

b) From Active Inclusion to Confrontation of Modalities Exclusion

At this stage, before developing other sections of this chapter, it is important to understand how traditionally individuals were benefitting from rights protection first within nation-states' constitutional systems and later through the concept of human rights. This will also shed more light on the idea of individuals as subject of international law, including international constitutionalism. The main keyword in this regard is that of citizenship: 'The citizen is the core unit of the constitutional order and of constitutional identity.'[29] The concept of citizenship is highly relevant to international law's approach to the place of individuals because of the continuing mediating role of states as explained in the previous section. For the purposes of our study, it is not necessary to look at different theories and understandings of citizenship. Addressing the legal regulation of citizenship within various domestic systems would also go beyond the framework of this study. This section focuses on the mechanisms that are activated when different groups of people get the entitlement to claim rights by virtue of being citizens of a particular state. More specifically, the contradiction highlighted by several authors between the universalist appeal of constitutional rights that theoretically postulate the equal worth of all human beings and the practical operation of constitutional rights protection that necessarily excludes many humans from its realm needs to be considered in light of the global constitutionalist project.[30] This contradiction or tension creates a specific exclusion/inclusion dynamic for which Etienne Balibar has developed a particularly insightful framework of analysis.

[29] Rosenfeld, *Identity*, 211.

[30] Ibid., 214; Balibar, *Citoyens d'Europe?*, for example 101–105. The English translation *People of Europe* does not exactly correspond to the contents of the French edition as some essays were dropped, others added. Therefore, some references are to the original French edition.

First, Balibar highlights how in order to resolve this tension, modern nation-states – and I would say with them also human rights law – adopt specific visions of equality that allow them to justify certain exclusions.[31] He distinguishes three modes of exclusion operated within different polities. Thus, in antiquity the exclusion operated by including and isolating e.g. women, children, slaves within the domestic or private sphere that was placed outside of equality.[32] The modern nation-state with its proclamations of rights excludes 'by *denaturating* those reputed incapable of autonomous judgment, that is, by inventing *anthropological alterity*, whose major variables are sex, race, morality, health and physical or mental age'.[33] Finally, the contemporary national-social state operates exclusion by disaffiliating those who were progressively included.[34] Thus, the mechanism that allows individuals to claim rights is based on the very possibility of excluding some from the benefit of rights. Therefore, relying on this same mechanism at the global level will not lead to the expected results. In particular the universality of human rights will always remain an unfulfilled promise. As long as human rights and international law more broadly rely on states and thus reinsert the exclusion/inclusion dynamic into their operation, individuals will be instrumentalised and some treated arbitrarily. Therefore, what is required is a move away from the exclusion/inclusion dynamic, not towards more inclusion but towards the dismantling of that very exclusion/inclusion dynamic. Balibar proposes a theoretical framework that can be viewed as a first step into this direction. A deeper questioning of this exclusion/inclusion dynamic continues in the part addressing the political in international constitutionalism.

Since all the struggles for inclusion into a given community lead only to the creation of new forms and mechanisms of exclusion, Balibar calls for a rethinking of the notion of community itself in a way that the very logic of exclusion/inclusion will become inoperative. In developing his thoughts on this proposal, Balibar draws on the works of Nancy and Rancière. Balibar takes from Nancy the notion of 'community without community' or 'community without a communal work'. This community

[31] Balibar, *Citoyens d'Europe?* 104–105. [32] Balibar, *People of Europe*, 66.
[33] Ibid., 68, emphasis in the original.
[34] Ibid., 68–69. This threefold vision of exclusion in Balibar mirrors Luhmann's three entry points for understanding exclusion/inclusion depending on the form of differentiation of society: segmented, stratified or functionally differentiated (Luhmann, 'Inklusion', 240–247). This similarity is important because Luhmann's theory forms the basis of the discussion of the functioning of human rights in Chapter 2.

without community is best understood through a distinction between communion and communication. Community without community emerges when communication (to which Nancy attributes a particular meaning) replaces communion.

> Communication consists before all else in this sharing and this compearance [com-parution] of finitude: that is, in the dislocation and in the interpellation that reveal themselves to be constitutive of being-in-common – precisely inasmuch as being-in-common is not a common being.[35]

This communication that exposes singularities, singular beings is opposed to the understanding of communication as a link, as a social bound that socially imposes a generality and then divides it. The sharing that Nancy emphasises in this community without community and in this communication 'does not divide up a pre-existing generality . . . but rather articulates singularities among themselves'.[36] This community is not totalisable, is not a unity in a traditional sense, but has as its function exposing of the 'irreducable human project of being "through one another"': 'The community experiences its greatest capacity to represent the common in the inclusion of the widest difference.'[37]

To arrive at his proposal Balibar continues with the work of Rancière, especially his *Disagreement: Politics and Philosophy*.[38] Here the guiding idea is Rancière's understanding of the political, more specifically of the political citizenship as a constitution and re-constitution of a people or *demos* through making a part of 'those who have no part':

> Politics exists when the natural order of domination is interrupted by the institution of a part of those who have no part. This institution is the whole of politics as a specific form of connection. It defines the common of the community as a political community, in other words, as divided, as based on a wrong that escapes the arithmetic of exchange and reparation. Beyond this set-up there is no politics. There is only the order of domination or the disorder of revolt.[39]

Combining these two insights – from Nancy and Rancière – Balibar proposes his own vision of citizenship and community. He affirms, '*it is always the practical confrontation with the different modalities of exclusion . . . that constitutes the founding moment of citizenship.*'[40] This movement of constituting citizenship, which is a continuous movement, can be presented

[35] Nancy as cited in Balibar, *People of Europe*, 70. [36] Ibid., 71 quoting Nancy.
[37] Ibid. [38] Rancière, *Disagreement.* [39] Ibid., 11–12.
[40] Balibar, *People of Europe*, 76, emphasis in the original.

> neither as a simple demand for inclusion (admission to a "club") on the part of those who, for one reason or another, have been excluded, nor as a humanitarian initiative on the part of those who see civic universalism as the source of legitimacy of their own rights. It must be the *common operation* or, if you prefer, the *"shared" act* of both – for example, those "with" and those "without" (papers, citizenship) . . . [41]

One important aspect of this vision is the emphasis on the constant re-constitution of community, not only through the capacity of those 'without' to become active citizens but also for those who nominally are already citizens to become citizens again by exercising 'once again their capacities in some way other than in a nominal fashion, by heritage and delegation'.[42]

This vision of citizenship that is focused on a constant re-constitution of the community is not opposed to the extension of the citizenship to the global level. To the contrary, it calls for a constant extension beyond borders both geographical and other more imaginary but no less real borders of identity, class, gender, race, sex and so on. To constantly renegotiate the borders of citizenship and confront exclusion becomes the very essence of citizenship. However, this comes coupled with a radical rethinking of our current political and legal practices, including those firmly embedded in international law. It also calls for the very difficult task of abandoning our traditionally liberal ways of thinking about many foundational notions such as equality, democracy, rights or politics. Some of these notions and the directions into which they have to be rethought will be addressed in the remainder of this study. At this stage, I will highlight onc important short-term consequence for international law: the need to recognise a more active role for individual human beings as such immediately at the international law level without the mediality of the states. In this sense the aim identified here is similar to the one advanced by Anne Peters discussed above and to the aspirations of many supporters of global constitutionalism. However, the position presented here differs in its emphasis on two aspects. First is my insistence on the fact that, so far, we are still far away from this immediate relevance of individuals at the level of international law. The second relates to the proposed ways of achieving this immediate relevance and active role for individuals.

The critical point that could radically change the position of individuals in international law, and thus create conditions for a global expansion of citizenship in the sense proposed by Balibar, relates to the role of individuals in law-making and law enforcement. Beyond simply being

[41] Ibid., 76–77, emphasis in the original. [42] Ibid., 76.

objects of protection and care, and thus objectified and instrumentalised by international law, there is a need to open up a space and opportunities for each human being to be able to actively engage with international law issues beyond a simply nominal role and beyond delegation. In order to illustrate this point, I will use the example of private sponsorship of refugees programme. I use this example not as an absolutely perfect model to be followed everywhere but as a seed, a place of inspiration where we can see some important elements at work that, if developed further, can allow human beings to assume for the first time an active role at the level of international law and thus create opportunities and conditions for an effective expansion of citizenship in the previously presented sense.

c) Private Sponsorship of Refugees as a Confrontation of Modalities of Exclusion[43]

Traditionally, the responsibility for fulfilling the obligations following form the Geneva Convention Relating to the Status of Refugees[44] and its Protocol[45] is the responsibility of states on whose territory a particular person claims asylum. However, taking into account the general reluctance of states to fulfil their obligations in this regard, which became particularly evident with what is usually called the 'migration crisis', as well as the wide discrepancy between and discretion enjoyed by different states in implementing these obligations, obtaining protection based on the claim to refugee status becomes very challenging. One of the alternative practices that allows people fleeing prosecution to get an adequate level of protection is the so-called private sponsorship of refugees. Within this framework, private entities, including individuals, can be active in fulfilling the international obligation of granting substitute protection that has been traditionally associated exclusively with states. Private sponsorship exists today in a few countries in various forms that allow individuals more or less freedom in actively fulfilling the obligation to grant protection.[46] Here, I will discuss only one historical example that best illustrates the idea of individuals as active immediately at the

[43] Some ideas presented in this section are developed in more detail in Yahyaoui Krivenko, 'Hospitality and Sovereignty'.

[44] Convention Relating to the Status of Refugees (Geneva Convention), 28 July 1951, UNTS, vol. 189, 137

[45] Protocol Relating to the Status of Refugees (Protocol), 31 January 1967, UNTS, vol. 606, 267

[46] For a recent overview of private sponsorship programmes see Kumin, *Welcoming Engagement* in general, and at 3–4, various forms and initiatives in different countries are listed.

international-law level as law enforcers and law-makers that could be regarded as a first step towards the emergence of the continuous movement of constituting citizenship and confronting the modalities of exclusion in the sense advocated by Balibar.

The example that will be discussed formed part of the Canadian private sponsorship of refugees programme until the revision of the Immigration and Refugee Protection Act[47] in 2011. The Canadian private sponsorship programme still functions, but without this particular category that will be used as an example. In general, private sponsorship is distinguished from governmental sponsorship programmes.[48] It allows private entities, such as incorporated or unincorporated entities or associations, but most importantly groups of at least five Canadian citizens or permanent residents to bring to Canada a refugee or a person in a refugee-like situation.[49] Within this latter category of persons in a refugee-like situation, the possibility to grant protection through resettlement could previously also extend to persons who had not yet left their country of origin but who otherwise fell under the 1951 Convention's definition of a refugee or who were 'being seriously and personally affected by civil war or armed conflict in that country', or who had been or were 'being detained or imprisoned with or without charges, or subjected to some other form of penal control, as a direct result of an act committed outside Canada that would, in Canada, be a legitimate expression of freedom of thought or a legitimate exercise of civil rights pertaining to dissent or trade union activity'.[50] Their country of origin or habitual residence had to be on the list created according to rules formulated in the IRPR.[51]

[47] Immigration and Refugee Protection Act, LC 2001, c-27 (IRPA).

[48] Governmental sponsorship of refugees is a more widely known and practiced phenomenon. It forms part of one of the durable solutions for refugees, namely resettlement (see e.g. UNHCR, 'Framework for Durable Solutions for Refugees and Persons of Concern', May 2003, in particular paras 12–16). 'Resettlement involves the selection and transfer of refugees from a State in which they have sought protection to a *third State which has agreed to admit them* – as refugees – with permanent residence status' (UNHCR, 'Resettlement Handbook', November 2004, I/2, emphasis added). This means that the *government* provides necessary administrative and material resources to enable the resettlement.

[49] The minimum duration of this undertaking is twelve months (Immigration and Refugee Protection Regulations (IRPR), SOR/2002-227, 154(2)). The duration of the undertaking can be more than one year, but should not exceed three years (IRPR 154(3)). Sponsorship includes financial responsibilities, as well as general assistance to help the person to successfully settle in the community (see e.g. IRPR 153(1) a) and b), 154(1) b)).

[50] IRPR, s 148(1) in its previous version, the so-called source country class.

[51] See, in particular, previous s 148(2) and 149 IRPR. The countries that are considered 'source countries' were listed in schedule 2. Lastly, six countries were set out in this

This means that five individuals coming together could grant protection to a person who otherwise would just fall through the cracks of the net of international obligations undertaken by states. In particular, the removal of the requirement to cross an international border is significant because many individuals whose life, personal integrity or other rights are targeted and violated simply do not have the opportunity to flee to another country. Equally significant is the extension of the circle of persons who can be protected beyond the narrow refugee definition. These two factors, combined with the fact that the undertaking for protection comes from a group of five individuals in another country, are a good example of how individuals can become active in enforcing and implementing international law and, in doing so directly, participate in international law-making through a contribution to practice as an element of custom. Obviously this example can lead to a paradigm shift only if this model is as much as possible removed from state control and extended to other areas of international law (e.g. initially by placing it under the auspices of the UNHCR). In the current state of international law, the very operation of the private sponsorship programme is dependant on the will of states. The suppression of the above-discussed possibility by the Canadian government is the best example. However, this example demonstrates the potential of active involvement of individuals with typically international law issues that goes beyond the traditional framework where individuals are recipients of rights or obligations upon which they do not decide. At the same time in this example we can also see how 'citizens' (or more precisely those who benefit from universal human rights) can fight for a redefinition of the boundaries of community and confront the modalities of exclusion of those who are yet outside of the protective framework of international law. Obviously, this process needs to simultaneously and actively engage both sides in order to not become an act of benevolent humanitarianism. However, it provides a good prototype of what 'the practical confrontation with the different modalities of exclusion (...) that constitutes the founding moment of citizenship'[52] could look like at the global level.

Thus, this section demonstrates that the predominant paradigm of individuals within international constitutionalism is still very instrumental: while placing individuals at the centre of its preoccupations, it

schedule: Colombia, El Salvador, Guatemala, Democratic Republic of Congo, Sierra Leone and Sudan.

52 Balibar, *People of Europe*, 76 as discussed in the previous section.

does not actually allow individuals to become active in defining their own place and the world around them. This is linked to the traditional mechanisms through which individuals claim rights within and beyond nation-states. The nation-state model of citizenship based on the exclusion/inclusion dynamic necessarily leads to the instrumentalisation and objectification of individuals as well as arbitrariness in the treatment of the excluded. This model of citizenship also continues to shape the functioning of human rights and international law more broadly because of the persistent mediation by states in international law. The theory of citizenship as a continual practical confrontation with the modalities of exclusion advanced by Balibar provided a theoretical foundation for thinking more creatively about the place of the individual with global constitutionalist goals in mind. The example from the Canadian private sponsorship of refugees programme was used as prototype of how a paradigm shift within the vision of the place of individuals in global constitutionalism could be achieved. As we have seen within the context of this example, overcoming state mediality remains one of the major steps required for the paradigm shift to happen. Therefore, as announced, the next part of this chapter will examine the place of states in theories of global constitutionalism.

2 *States in Global Constitutionalism*

a) Overview of Current Debates in International Constitutionalism

The ideas about constitutionalism and constitutionalisation elaborated by international lawyers are influenced by their professional identity and self-representation as specialists of *international* law. Since states remain the main subjects of international law, it is difficult for any international lawyer to disregard states or even to imagine how life could be organised at a global scale if states disappear.[53] A more acceptable route leads proponents of global or international constitutionalism into recognition of and emphasis on the changing nature and role of states at the international arena. They readily recognise that states become less relevant and less powerful. They also usually readily admit the multiplicity of actors that intervene in the everyday functioning of international law.

A helpful starting point for understanding the role and status of states within global constitutionalism is the position clearly articulated and

[53] See e.g. Marks, 'State Centrism'.

detailed by Anne Peters, one of the main and widely published mainstream advocates of international constitutionalism. Nuances of opinions expressed by other authors will then be introduced against this background, where available. The starting point is the recognition that international law is not conceived today as 'pure and exclusively inter-state law',[54] thus acknowledging the presence and importance of other subjects of international law. The second movement is 'a shift of perspective' that views the status of states as subjects of international law that are equivalent in status to other subjects of international law despite the privileged position of states, for instance as principal creators of international law. As Peters puts it, 'this is a technical status only'.[55] According to her, the status and legitimacy of states as subjects of international law 'depend on how they serve individuals as members of humanity'.[56] The ensuing discussion by Peters oscillates between the assessment of the current status of states in international law and their desired future role, placing emphasis on two issues: responsibility to protect and equality of states. The responsibility to protect is conceptualised as an obligation that changes the nature of the state's personality and facilitates the placing of individuals at the centre of concerns of international law.[57] Formal equality between states is utilised as a starting point for a discussion about possible future developments towards a more complex substantive understanding of equality, for example paying attention to population size within states or to states' respect 'for the most basic human rights'.[58] In all scenarios states are firmly part of the constitutionalisation project. However, in order to reconcile their powers and dominant position with the need to push individuals into the centre of the constitutionalised international system, all the powers are relativised through a simple shift in perspective. This shift in perspective on the status of states as subjects of international law also involves a change in the conceptualisation of sovereignty as an essential attribute of statehood. In this vision of states, the change in perspective on sovereignty signifies that sovereignty is not regarded as a privilege or absolute power. It becomes defined as a bundle of rights and obligations.[59]

Significantly, in this vision of the international legal system, states remain essential mediators without which individual human beings cannot be placed at the centre of the constitutionalised international

[54] Klabbers, Peters and Ulfstein, *Constitutionalization*, 180. [55] Ibid. [56] Ibid.
[57] Ibid., 186–189. [58] Ibid., 196, and more generally, 191–197.
[59] Ibid., 182–185. In addition to Peters this opinion is clearly outlined by Fassbender, 'Sovereignty and Constitutionalism'.

system. Thus, the role and function of states can be visualised through the image of interlocked gears in a complex mechanism. This mechanism can be put to different uses, for example to move a belt, a chain, or a rope that in turn can move or effect change in something else. The mechanism can be adapted to different uses and designed in a way that gears become almost or entirely invisible. When we study and design improvements to this mechanism, we can focus on belts, chains and other elements around gears or we can focus on gears. However, the mechanism will not function without the gears. We can say that this centrality of gears to the mechanism is a privilege or a bundle of functions (rights and obligations) that the gears fulfil for chains, belts and other elements. This however, does not mean that the mechanism will be fundamentally different. The change in perspective on the mechanism and its parts does not create a new mechanism. Whatever the perspective, chains can be replaced by belts, belts can be replaced by ropes, etc., but gears remain central elements. The mainstream vision of international constitutionalism attempts to put a particular type of belt, or chain, or rope around gears, and to disguise gears so that they are less visible and more attention is paid to belts and chains. However, gears remain in place as central elements without which the mechanism they put in place will not be able to function. Thus, the indissoluble link between the fate of human rights and the fate of the modern nation-state 'in such a way that the waning of the latter necessarily implies the obsolescence of the former'[60] remains central. The movement of international constitutionalism even reinforces this link between states and human rights.

Other scholars working within the intellectual tradition of global or international constitutionalism do not articulate their view on the role of states as clearly. However, the implied paradigm in relation to states is the same or very similar to the view presented above. For example, any author approaching the issue of constitutionalisation of international law through the lens of the UN Charter necessarily accepts the underlying premises that make states central actors of the UN system.[61]

[60] Agamben, 'Beyond Human Rights', 92 with reference to Arendt, *The Origins of Totalitarianism*, in particular the content and title of the section entitled 'The Decline of the Nation-State and the End of the Rights of Man'.

[61] The most prominent representative of this stream in international constitutionalism is Fassbender. See e.g. Fassbender, *Charter as the Constitution*, Fassbender, 'Rediscovering a Forgotten Constitution'; Fassbender, 'The United Nations Charter'. Some of the other authors addressing the topic include Doyle, 'The UN Charter'; Frank, 'Is the UN Charter a Constitution?'; Macdonald, 'The United Nations Charter'.

Similarly, ideas about international constitutionalism that revolve around different sources of international law without questioning the nature and processes of the source's creation, or without questioning the privileged position of states as law-makers, maintain the centrality of states within the constitutionalised vision of international law.[62]

Thus, international constitutionalists approach states with care. While they are conscious of the privileged position of states and attempt to reconcile it with the centrality of individuals they postulate as one of the main characteristics of global constitutionalism, they also would maintain that

> We should not be too quick to abandon our concepts (sovereignty, sovereign equality, international law and so on).... [D]espite the expanding regulatory roles of global governance institutions, increased integration of the international community (and of regional communities) does not amount to the end of sovereign territorial states.[63]

Thus, again we can see a sort of an oscillation between the need to reconsider the position of the state accommodating the diversity of actors at the global arena and utilisation of the position of states.[64]

The centrality of states is further confirmed by the fact that, in the discourse of international lawyers, the term 'sovereignty' remains a characteristic attached almost exclusively to states.[65] There are authors who insist on the sovereignty of people, especially in the context of the right to self-determination and the rights of indigenous people.[66] However, all other entities that we can encounter at the level of international law are

62 See for example De Wet's value-oriented version of international constitutionalism. Here values come from *jus cogens*, human rights, *erga omnes* and thus from states. She also mentions that states are *ex officio* members of the international community: De Wet, 'International Constitutional Order', 56. Similarly, the view of international constitutionalism as being based on general principles of law advanced by Kadelbach and Kleinlein implies the dominant position of states. This is particularly clear when they connect the proposal to the theory of sources: Kadelbach and Kleinlein, 'International Law'. Another example is the argument developed by Petersen that constitutionalisation can be identified in the type of custom that does not require state practice. However, the *opinion juris* element is still linked back to states, for instance in the reference to the UN General Assembly resolutions and other methods of identifying consensus: Petersen, 'Wandel des ungeschriebenen Völkerrechts'.

63 Cohen, 'Constitutionalism', 129.

64 See similar conclusion in O'Donoghue, 'International Constitutionalism and the State', 1045.

65 In addition to the exception mentioned in the next sentence, we should not forget the Sovereign Military Hospitaller Order of Saint John of Jerusalem of Rhodes and of Malta.

66 See e.g. Araujo, 'Sovereignty'; Lenzerini, 'Sovereignty Revisited'.

defined as autonomous, self-contained, perhaps even independent but never sovereign. On the other hand, in the philosophical discourse it is not uncommon to define the individual human being as sovereign.[67] This highlights the peculiar privileged although constantly mutating place of states. At the same time, this use of the term 'sovereignty' brings to light a paradox: the term sovereignty is applied to the most powerful actor within a particular arena (the state), but it can also characterise the most disempowered actor (the individual). This in turn establishes a connection between two paradigms, the paradigm of the state and the paradigm of the individual that is explored in more detail in subsequent chapters. However, the question remains whether it is possible to overcome the state in thinking about the ordering of the global and in particular about global constitutionalism.

Some authors attempted to develop alternative visions of the structuring tendencies at the international level. These alternative visions are based on the main premise that the contemporary international system clearly moves beyond the state and their sovereignty. Within this alternative strand of international legal scholarship, two main camps can be identified: societal constitutionalism and normative/legal pluralism. The most prominent representative of societal constitutionalism as applied to the global realm is Gunther Teubner.[68] He demonstrates that constitutional structures arise within various autonomous social sectors, not only states. According to Teubner, these non-state constitutions are fundamental to understanding contemporary globalisation processes.

The scholarship on legal and normative pluralism is very rich and divers. The intersection of two aspects in this literature is of interest when considering the role of states in constitutionalisation processes at the global level: how legal and normative pluralism attempts to move beyond the state and how pluralism in moving beyond the state approaches the ordering of the global. From this perspective, advocates

[67] This is particularly prominent in discussions drawing on Nietzsche, see e.g. Leiter, 'Who Is the "Sovereign Individual"?'. The theme was also extensively theorised by Derrida, in particular in Derrida, *Rogues*, 137–138. For an interesting analysis of Derrida on this issue see Mansfield, *God Who Deconstructs Himself.*

[68] The main reference point for this aspect of Teubner's work remains Teubner, *Constitutional Fragments.* Some other important contributions from Teubner on the topic include Teubner, 'Global Bukowina' and Teubner, 'Societal Constitutionalism'. It should be noted that other authors also theorised the idea of societal constitutionalism. Initially, it was developed in Sciulli, *Theory of Societal Constitutionalism.* The most recent work that uses the concept of societal constitutionalism in relation to the global is Kjaer, *Constitutionalism.*

of 'postnational' pluralist legal order make the most intriguing claim.[69] This claims entails a possibility of conceiving a legal order beyond the state. The degree of success of attempts made by the proponents of either societal constitutionalism or postnational legal pluralism to escape the state will be discussed in the next section.

b) State Thinking as a Structuring Device

The main argument developed in this section is that even when alternative forms of global governance are envisaged – like societal constitutionalism or postnational pluralism – the fundamental structuring processes are those that we inherited and learned from the state. Thus the state survives and dictates how we think about processes taking place and possible reforms at the global level. Therefore, it will be argued that other ways of overcoming the state need to be developed. The second part of this section will clarify why the state needs to be overcome in thinking about global constitutionalism and will propose some strategies.

In order to defend this thesis and its implications for thinking about global constitutionalism, the work on the notion of state by French sociologist Pierre Bourdieu will be used. Bourdieu's primary interest in sociology was not the state. His writings on the notion of state as such represent only a marginal part of his work. However, he did deliver a series of lectures on the state[70] and subsequently published some ideas presented in the lectures in the form of articles.[71] His interest in such issues as evolution of modes of domination, division of social labour in domination, but also educational systems and cultural practices led him to a particular understanding of the notion of state that he presented in his teaching at Collège de France between 1989 and 1991. The transcripts of these lectures were published in French in 2012.

The discussion below starts with the presentation of Bourdieu's ideas about the state as they emerge from his lectures at Collège de France. This vision is obviously based on his previous work so references to Bourdieu's works that are relevant for particular issues discussed are also incorporated. Another important disclaimer relates to the fact that this summary focuses on characteristics of the state identified by

69 For an overview of the discussion of different 'postnational' positions in scholarly debates see Walker, 'Postnational Constitutionalism'.

70 Bourdieu, *Sur l'État*. All subsequent references are primarily to the original French edition. Where appropriate, a page number of the English edition is given in parenthesis.

71 See in particular Bourdieu, 'Esprits d'Etat'; and Bourdieu, 'De la maison du roi a la raison d'Etat'.

Bourdieu that then can be used for analysis of an international lawyer's thinking on global constitutionalism and the role of states. Therefore, at times emphasis is placed on aspects that another reader of Bourdieu, in particular a sociologist, might find less significant or central. Finally, this is just a summary of very complex thinking that was built and has evolved over years. Bourdieu himself on several occasions makes a number of disclaimers emphasising that he simplifies a lot of issues and that he cannot possibly provide a full picture, only a simplified model of the logic of the state constituting itself.[72]

(1) Bourdieu's Methodological Remarks Bourdieu starts by explaining in quite a lot of detail his particular approach to the notion of the state. This approach is described as genetic history.[73] The specific difficulty he identifies in dealing with the notion of the state relates to his acknowledgement of the fact that the state structures our thinking. How can we think about the state without being unconsciously directed and influenced by the state? How can we avoid 'de penser l'État avec une pensée d'État'? he asks constantly.[74] This question serves as a reminder to avoid to 'projeter dans l'objet, sur l'objet, sa propre pensée de l'objet qui est précisément le produit de l'objet'.[75] His insistence on this point becomes clear with the development of his arguments. At this stage it is important to clarify his approach, which he views as indispensable for any person approaching the state,[76] because it represents one of the major instruments of rupture.[77] He uses this instrument to evade or suspend all the presuppositions that are engaged in an enquiry due to the fact that our thinking is also a product of what we think and study.[78] The three essential elements of his approach are empirical analysis, critique of the theoretical presuppositions of current theories, and questioning of the formulation of dominant problems.[79] However, his genetic history represents an additional way, and the most powerful according to him, to confront the state thinking ('pensée d'État' in French').[80]

[72] Bourdieu, *Sur l'État*, 294.

[73] Ibid., 169ff. (105ff.) in particular but also 143ff. (86ff.) on genetic structuralism. He also emphasises the difference between his approach and genealogy in the Foucauldian sense: Ibid., 185 (115).

[74] Ibid., for example 171, translated into English as 'thinking the state with state thinking' (106) but the original French sentence is more expressive.

[75] Ibid., 'projecting onto the object, into the object, one's own thinking about the object which is precisely the product of the object itself'.

[76] Ibid., 170 (106). [77] Ibid., 171 (106). [78] Ibid., 172 (107). [79] Ibid., 183 (114–115).

[80] Ibid.

In essence, genetic history signifies a return to the uncertainty attached to the beginning when something started, a point when it is possible to discover the infinity of possibilities attached to this uncertainty.[81] This infinity of possibilities disappears with time, it is forgotten, and the result that we know (for instance the state) is taken for granted ('that's how it is'). In order to question this obviousness of certain structures, of which the state is the most powerful one, we need to destroy the 'doxa', a belief that does not recognise itself as such, is not aware of itself as such,[82] and rediscover all these other possibilities.

Employing his strategy in relation to the idea of the state, Bourdieu goes through a series of demonstrations of particular characteristics of the state as they appear through the emergence process of the state. Below I sketch this process (Bourdieu says 'constitution' of the state) and the main characteristics of the state as described by Bourdieu.

(2) Constitution of the State According to Bourdieu state emerges or constitutes itself ('*se constitue*' the term Bourdieu constantly uses in French) through the concentration of different types of capital accompanied by a process of transmutation.[83] Bourdieu highlights that this accumulation is not a simple addition or sum of these capitals because it is always accompanied by changes that emerge as a result of accumulation.[84] Bourdieu uses the notion of capital differently from the Marxist tradition, where this notion has an exclusively economic, material connotation. Bourdieu identifies a series of types of capital that need to be accumulated for a state to constitute itself: economic, physical force, symbolic, cultural and informational.[85] While Bourdieu presents accumulation of these types of capital one by one, he emphasises that this contradicts the logic of the emergence of the state, an entity that is irreducible to the sum of the elements that constitute it.[86] In the process of accumulation and transmutation, symbolic capital occupies a central place because this type of capital is born out of the interaction between

[81] Ibid., 186 (115). [82] Ibid., 188 (117). [83] Ibid., 294 (191). [84] Ibid., 295 (191).

[85] For a specific discussion for each type, see ibid., 300–304, 313–324, 335–341 and 357–362 (in English: 198–205, 209–211, 212–216; 229–232) but also generally the notion of symbolic capital is important for Bourdieu's discussion of symbolic violence or power. This will be presented in more detail below. Some of Bourdieu's works where the notion of symbolic capital is discussed include Bourdieu and Wacquant, 'Symbolic Capital and Social Classes'; Bourdieu, 'Le capital social'; Bourdieu, *Esquisse*, 348–376.

[86] Bourdieu, *Sur l'État*. 301 (197).

any type of capital and agents socialised to recognise this other type of capital.[87]

In constituting itself the state acquires certain characteristics, certain ways of existing and maintaining itself, that need to be comprehended. I identify three such characteristics that appear central to Bourdieu's discussion of the state: symbolic violence or power, the idea of the official or public space, and the idea of the universal. The latter two are discussed below together. These three characteristics are essential to our ability to take a renewed look at the alternative thinking about the global ordering in international law.

(3) Characteristics of the State

(a) Symbolic Violence/Power

In developing the idea of symbolic violence or symbolic power Bourdieu starts from Weber's definition of the state as a monopoly of the legitimate use of physical force.[88] However, he goes beyond this definition in adding that one of the essential characteristics of a state is its monopoly of the legitimate use of symbolic force or violence. Symbolic violence is defined as forms of constraint that are based on unconscious agreements between objective structures and mental structures.[89] Symbolic violence takes forms that are 'invisible' and is exercised in complicity with those who are subjected to this violence.[90] Bourdieu's work on symbolic violence, or more often he says symbolic power, is quite extensive and well-known, but initially it was not directly related to the notion of the state.[91]

In order to understand what Bourdieu means by symbolic violence, it is essential to link it to other ideas that led Bourdieu to the articulation of this notion. The notion of symbolic power or violence was born out of Bourdieu's effort to overcome the separation between objectivism and subjectivism – sometimes also named physicalism and psychologism – in social science.[92] Therefore, it is important not to conceptualise symbolic violence as somehow being only spiritual, unreal: 'Les rapports de force les plus brutaux (. . .) sont en meme temps des rapports symboliques.'[93] To clarify this, Bourdieu insists that all forms of brutal physical violence

87 Ibid., 302 (198). 88 Weber, 'Politik als Beruf', 397.

89 Bourdieu, *Sur l'État*, 239 (164). 90 Ibid.

91 See for example the volume *Language and Symbolic Power* where relevant works of Bourdieu translated into English are collected.

92 Bourdieu, 'Social Space', 14.

93 Bourdieu, *Sur l'État*, 260. 'The most brutal relationships of power are at the same time symbolic relationships' (author's translation).

affect people not only through the pure physical force but also because we attribute some symbolic value to these acts of physical force.

Institutions such as the state exist and function only if there is a correspondence, correlation between objective and subjective structures.[94] For example, the state exists twice: objectively in its material structures and institutions, and subjectively in mental structures and representations.[95] The symbolic order that the state constitutes by constituting itself simultaneously is imposed in these two forms that are interrelated. In doing so the state establishes coherence between these two sorts of structures, a coherence that then is regarded as natural, obvious (doxa). Thus, Bourdieu emphasises that any act of submission or obedience is also a cognitive act that implies cognition (knowledge) and recognition.[96] Cognition ('act de connaissance') is not the same as ordinary knowledge habitually understood. It is something that we learned unconsciously or learned and internalised so that it became unconscious. Bourdieu also uses the term 'corporeal knowledge' ('act de connaissance corporelle').[97] We can notice here how something that is traditionally viewed as being of the order of the subjective or spiritual (knowledge) becomes interwoven with something that is traditionally part of the objective or material (body). Thus, social structures and the state as a meta-structure are simultaneously and inseparably subjective and objective, reproducing and producing themselves through this production of both subjective and objective structures that condition each other.

For Bourdieu, in order to understand symbolic systems and symbolic power, it is equally essential to understand the role of agents who are engaged in the construction, contestations and other acts related to this symbolic system and symbolic power. With regard to the state Bourdieu particularly emphasises the role of jurists. He even affirms that jurists produced the state through their discourse and produced themselves as jurists in producing the state.[98] Most importantly, he identifies law as a quintessential form of symbolic power that is monopolised by the state.[99]

(b) Public/Official and Universal

The very existence of the state is intimately linked to the production of the official discourse. At the same time as some agents/official representatives

[94] Ibid., 263. [95] Ibid., 24. [96] Ibid., 260, 275 (173). [97] Ibid., 275–276 (173).

[98] Ibid., 95, 277 (175, 211). See also Bourdieu, 'La force du droit', in general; and Bourdieu, *La Noblesse d'État*, Chapter 4.

[99] Bourdieu, 'Force du droit', 3.

or simply scholars speak in the name of a particular entity (in our case the state), they make this entity existent.[100] Therefore, the predominant role of lawyers in producing and maintaining the state comes again to the forefront. The official is always pretending to be unanimously recognised and thus becomes the public. The official discourse is always a public discourse, as opposed to private, singular or hidden.[101] The official or public discourse as a characteristic of the state always produces the effect of universalisation.[102]

Universal is always at the same time *monopolisation* of the universal and *particularisation* because other incompatible visions, skills or knowledge are suppressed and eliminated.[103] The emergence of the state is linked to the monopolisation of the universal and emergence of the universal as a new form of resources.[104]

This brief overview of Bourdieu's examination of the state highlights some essential characteristics of the state but also cautions against a too hasty dismissal of the state, particularly because of the way we internalise state thinking. Therefore, it provides an efficient tool for examining theories attempting to go beyond the state. The goal is to determine how far we went on the road of overcoming state-centricity at the global level.

(4) Reading the Global with Bourdieu In this section one alternative theory of global constitutionalism and one proposed alternative to global constitutionalism are reread through the prism of Bourdieu's work on the notion of the state. The theories selected are intentionally those that claim to go beyond the state. The first theory is the theory of societal constitutionalism as articulated by Teubner in relation to the global realm.[105] The second theory is Krisch's plea for the recognition of postnational law and the associated argument in favour of pluralism.[106]

[100] Bourdieu, *Sur l'État*, 80 (40). [101] Ibid., 87, 91 (48). [102] Ibid., 87 (33).
[103] Ibid., 162–164 (100–101). [104] Ibid., 255, 163 (100).
[105] It should always be reminded that initially the theory of societal constitutionalism was developed by Sciulli (see note 68 above). This theory forms one of the four theoretical bases of Teubner's own work that is more properly described as 'a sociological theory of societal constitutionalism' (Teubner, *Constitutional Fragments*, 3). The other three bases are general theories of social differentiation, constitutional sociology and the theory of private government (Ibid.) However, for the sake of brevity, the term 'transnational societal constitutionalism' or simply 'societal constitutionalism' is used.
[106] The main reference here will be Krisch, *Beyond Constitutionalism*.

(a) Transnational Societal Constitutionalism

Teubner's idea of constitutionalisation of functional global regimes is an attempt to formulate an answer to the question of how constitutions could or should also govern non-state areas of society,[107] in particular in times of globalisation.[108] More specifically, based on Teubner's claim that societal constitutionalism existed within nation-states too, it is more appropriate to ask 'how can nation states' experiences with societal constitutionalism be transformed under the different conditions of globality?'[109]

Teubner claims that it is possible to transpose nation-states' constitutional experiences to other non-state social structures, or in other words to constitutionalise transnational regimes,[110] and that this is what is happening today in several functional areas. Thus, the main opposition that dominates Teubner's work is that between state constitutions and constitutions of transnational regimes as non-state entities. Bourdieu's description of states' emergence and the resulting characteristics of the state will allow us to affirm that these transnational regimes and their constitutionalisation are not qualitatively different from states. Therefore, the opposition between state and non-state constitutionalisation as articulated by Teubner is illusory. Due to the fact that constitutionalisation of these transnational functional regimes is at a very early stage of development and because a significant part of Teubner's analysis is hypothetical, it is difficult to provide a definitive diagnosis of his theory. I will argue that developments described by Teubner, depending on the precise shape they take in the future, can signal one of the two following directions: Either the transnational functional regimes are in the process of becoming new states with the reach of their competence being defined not territorially, like in the case of nation-states, but functionally; or the process of constitutionalisation of these regimes indicates that the process of differentiation of different types of capital in Bourdieu's sense is taking place globally, thus indicating the possibility of emergence of a global state.

Bourdieu's depiction of the emergence of states possesses striking parallels to Teubner's description of the transition from the constitutive phase to the limitative phase in the constitutional development of

[107] Teubner, *Constitutional Fragments*, 5. [108] Ibid., 6. [109] Ibid., 7.

[110] Transnational regime is defined by Teubner, with reference to Krasner (Stephen D. Krasner, 'Structural Causes and Regime Consequences: Regimes as Intervening Variables' (1982), 36, *International Organization*, 185–205), as a 'set of principles, norms, rules, and decision-making procedures around which actors' expectations converge in a given cause-area'. Teubner, *Constitutional Fragments*, 58.

transnational functional regimes. For instance, in his example of plain money regulation, the unrestricted growth prompted by private commercial banks and the ensuing need for self-constraint can be compared to the initial stage of concentration of different types of capital in the hands of the state. This initial concentration of different forms of capital in the hands of the state is, according to Bourdieu, simultaneously a concentration of the symbolic capital. The symbolic capital, as explained above, is essential in order for the state to be able to dispose of other forms of capital. In order to achieve this concentration of a particular form of capital in the hands of the state, double work needs to be accomplished according to Bourdieu: justification and institutionalisation (creation of institutions and functions that can legitimately act within this particular area in the name of the state, in Teubner's case in the name of the regime).[111] The work of justification within the framework of the emergence of the state is essentially accomplished by jurists who develop a number of reasons justifying why a state can have a particular power. We can see how Teubner and other authors quoted in this book, who justify the need for restraining power of private banks to produce plain money, perform precisely this type of justificatory work.[112] At the same time as justifying the central banks' prerogative to create money – in Bourdeu's terms it is a concentration of a particular form of capital – central banks become those legitimate institutions that can act in the name of the regime (state) with regard to this particular type of capital. By positioning central banks as reflexive bodies aimed at establishing the specific rationality and normativity of the social sphere and making them compatible with their environment,[113] Teubner and other proponents of societal constitutionalism perform the legitimating work jurists performed in the establishment of states, thus producing the required symbolic capital and creating possibilities for the exercise of symbolic power by the regimes.

Within the current framework, it is not possible to go into a deeper analysis of the many analogies existing between constitutionalisation of transnational functional regimes and the emergence and self-constitution of states. However, I highlight that the constitutionalisation process described by Teubner leads to a monopolisation of powers within a particular functional field similar to the monopolisation of powers within a particular territory by a state. Simultaneously, this leads to universalisation within this particular field (territory) of the discourse

[111] Bourdieu, *Sur l'État*, 327–328. [112] Teubner, *Constitutional Fragments*, 96–103.
[113] Ibid., 101.

of the legitimate institutions. Naturally, as Bourdieu demonstrates, there are always resistances, fluctuations, back and forth movements within these monopolising and universalising tendencies, but the general trend is clearly visible. Similarly to the processes of concentration and differentiation described by Bourdieu with regard to the emergence of the state, self-limitation and differentiation of regimes lead actually to their unification.

Obviously, since the limitation or the area of competence of regimes is functional, not territorial, the objection to the above analysis could be that regimes actually concentrate only on one form of capital, accompanied by a production of symbolic capital through the role of law since symbolic capital accompanies concentration of any type of capital. Two responses to this objection are possible. First, it is possible for regimes to have a functionally determined area of influence comparable to a territory of a state while accumulating within this area all required types of capital, therefore allowing the regime and its legitimate institutions to become the meta-field within the particular area. This would signify emergence of functional states. Another response could be to admit that constitutionalisation of transnational functional regimes is actually a form of concentration and differentiation of various forms of capital at the global level. This would imply that the societal constitutionalism in the form developed by Teubner actually describes initial stages of the emergence and self-constitution of a global state. Similarly to the initial stage of the state constituting itself through a differentiation and concentration of various forms of capital within a given territory, constitutionalisation of transnational regimes performs this differentiation and concentration at the global level. We need more time to see if this process will lead to the next stage when a global coordinating meta-field emerges, but this is not impossible if social systems tend to follow same patterns. In light of Teubner's own concluding consideration on the constitutional conflicts between different regimes and proposed ways of dealing with them, the analogy between regimes and states seems more obvious than the emergence of the global state.

The purpose of this brief analysis was not to question or dispute the diagnosis proposed by Teubner or the possible ways forward he formulated. The main objective was to demonstrate that state thinking ('pensée d'État') dominates his work, as it still does in the work of the majority of scholars writing on global, international or transnational issues. Despite his claim that regimes are non-state actors, Bourdieu's analysis of the state reveals how state structures and thinking remain central to the regimes. Equally, celebration of the pluralism, policentricity and heterarchy associated with the societal constitutionalism as applied to the global realm seems in this light too optimistic. At the final analysis, international law based on the nation-state systems was also characterised by the absence of hierarchy and coordination between a variety of actors that with time became more and more uniform and centralised. We have to await more advanced stages of development of these different regimes, societal structures and networks to see the precise shape they will take at the global level. Taking into account the centrality of state thinking to their current stage of development, it is not impossible that they will move in a direction very similar to the current state of public international law, simply focusing on functional, not territorial areas.

The main problem with concealing, even unwittingly, state thinking is that, as Bourdieu like many thinkers before him clearly demonstrates, the state always implies a relationship of domination. Monopolisation operated by a state in order to concentrate different forms of capital, necessarily marginalises and excludes all conflicting and undesirable views, opinions and possibilities. Even if the symbolic violence or power is not immediately visible, it still produces effects harming many human beings. And precisely because this domination and violence are so pervasive and invisible, scholars need to be more attentive and careful when affirming the end of the state or emergence of non-state entities.

(b) Postnational Pluralism

The idea of postnational law is the second example discussed in order to shed more light on the place of the state in the attempts to overcome the state in thinking about the global. The main point of reference in this discussion is Nico Krisch's work that articulates most clearly the idea of postnational law detached from constitutionalism.[114] As with the societal constitutionalism the main objective is not to challenge the analysis performed but to interrogate the overall framing of the issue as postnational. I will demonstrate that state thinking is still at play within this work that attempts to move beyond constitutionalism and beyond the state-centred experience of the West.

One of the central premises against which Krisch's thesis about postantional law is situated postulates that globalisation has transformed law and politics in ways that we have still yet to fully comprehend.[115] In attempting to clarify challenges posed by these transformations, Krisch focuses on

[114] Krisch, *Beyond Constitutionalism.* [115] Ibid., 4.

structural issues, rather than on the substance of the law.[116] He identifies two main contrasting structural visions – postnational constitutionalism[117] and pluralism – and inquires into their respective virtues from a theoretical and a practical perspective.[118] From the outset Krisch favours pluralism, which he associates with openness, heterogeneity and heterarchy, positioning these attributes as absent or less present in constitutionalism. He also affirms that 'pluralism eschews a central element of the Western political tradition – the hope to constrain politics through the rule of law.'[119] Postnational pluralism is difficult to define if it is not placed in opposition to constitutionalism.[120]

It is equally important to highlight that Krisch's rejection of constitutionalism as applied to the global realm is based on quite a narrow reading of constitutionalism, namely one that is faithful to the experience of the domestic political legitimacy of Western states over the last two centuries.[121] He rejects certain visions and rereadings of constitutionalism as being not 'constitutional' enough, as departing too far from this tradition.[122] Therefore, from the outset, the duality between constitutionalism and pluralism that Krisch establishes is artificially constructed. This artificially constructed opposition between constitutionalism and pluralism makes Krisch's arguments in favour of pluralism appear more persuasive. A selective picture of pluralism reinforces this duality and artificiality. Chapter 3 of Krisch's book presents the framework of pluralism and draws mainly on relatively recent literature focused on global pluralism with a strong European dimension. However, the history of legal pluralism is much older and more complex. Krisch mentions this briefly in passing.[123] In particular, historically, the idea of legal pluralism emerged within domestic nation-state settings. On several occasions Krisch deplores constitutionalism's domestic analogy and emphasises that the contemporary global world needs a new structure.[124] However,

[116] Ibid., 23.
[117] Although he uses the term postnational constitutionalism, what he broadly has in mind is what is discussed here as global or international constitutionalism.
[118] Krisch, *Beyond Constitutionalism*, 23–25. [119] *Ibid.*, 23.
[120] For example, when summarising the analysis of postnational pluralism, Krisch states, 'Postnational pluralism recognizes the blurred separation of layers of law but does not seek to reorganize them in an overarching legal framework, as does constitutionalism.' Ibid., 298.
[121] Ibid., 40.
[122] See in particular his rejection of James Tully's notion of 'common constitutionalism' (Ibid., 40), other examples at 39–40.
[123] Ibid., 72. [124] Ibid., 35, 69.

legal pluralism also has strong historical ties to nation-states and is based on domestic analogy. Most disturbingly perhaps, the 'classical legal pluralism' is tied to the colonisation experience and European imposition of its legal standards in many parts of the world.[125] Krisch does not mention this historical experience of legal pluralism, although in the part on constitutionalism he insists that in order to translate a concept from one context to another, one of the essential steps consist in 'a detailed engagement with the history of the concept, with its different historical understandings and the varying degrees of appeal they have had over time'.[126] Without a detailed discussion, Krisch simply mentions only some of these historical ties between pluralism and domestic context, for example pluralism within the context of the early practice and theory of federalism,[127] but they do not seem to be so disturbing to him as in the case of constitutionalism. Over time different visions of pluralism have been developed, some overcoming quite successfully the initial link to the state. Similar efforts exist within constitutionalist thinking. However, as stated above, Krisch does not recognise them.

The choice of terminology produces significant influences on the dominant perception of both terms. Constitutionalism that is associated with nation-states makes the thinking of the state apparent and perhaps too prominent as compared to the actual content of various theories of constitutionalism. The term pluralism works in the opposite direction: It allows an easier semblance of a rupture with state thinking and actually makes state thinking invisible without making it non-existent, without avoiding it. Thus, Krisch's enthusiasm for pluralism and his insistence on pluralism's ability to leave the state-centred structures behind might be exaggerated if we take more seriously the state-related pedigree of pluralism. Beyond these linguistic choices, Krisch also uses a series of examples to illustrate the virtues of pluralism over constitutionalism. However, state thinking is present at this level too.

One of the main framing devices in Krisch's book is the idea of postnational law. The choice of the term is symptomatic of the desire to produce something new, something different from the traditional international law that operates in a state-centred framework. However, the most sticking feature of this postnational law is that its main actors,

125 See two particularly powerful articles on this topic, both published in the 1980s when new forms of legal pluralism started to emerge and being advocated: Griffiths, 'What Is Legal Pluralism?' and Merry, 'Legal Pluralism'.

126 Krisch, *Beyond Constitutionalism*, 38.

127 Ibid., 72

institutions and decision-makers are either states or state-empowered and state-made institutions.

Krisch's own understanding of the term 'postnational' is formulated as follows: 'The national sphere retains importance, but is no longer the paradigmatic anchor of the whole order.'[128] Another important element of what he characterises as postnational law is its articulation in an increasingly blurred distinction between the domestic and international spheres.[129] Against the backdrop of this characterisation of the postnational, it should be highlighted that connections between domestic and international law have always existed. However, for quite a long period of time these connections disappeared and still disappear sometimes today in their *conceptualisation* by some international lawyers.[130] Interestingly, research shows that at least some lawyers who defended this dualism between domestic and international law were aware of the artificiality of the distinction.[131] Their insistence was motivated by the need to concentrate symbolic resources that would allow the field of international law to emerge as a unified discipline able to speak in the name of the universal. The need to resort to the language of postnational law can be indicative of very similar desires but directed this time towards a creation of a discipline and a cognitive framework that can establish itself as independent from international law, mainly through its claim to overcome the state

At this stage we need to recall what Bourdieu said about the role of jurists in the emergence of the state. According to Bourdieu juridical capital is the symbolic capital *par excellence*, and jurists contributed to the construction of the state through their capacity to use appropriate linguistic forms and present their discourse as universal while particularising.[132] Adopting Bourdieu's prism, we can ask a series of additional questions: Where does the legitimacy of all those institutions Krisch mentions in his work come from? Who appoints the people who compose those institutions? Who delivers to them diplomas and qualifications that everybody considers as making them eligible for these positions? In the overwhelming majority of cases, if not all, the answer will be the state. For example, who educates, delivers diplomas and elects or appoints judges in domestic courts that occupy a prominent place in

[128] Ibid., 4. [129] Ibid., 4 and 302.

[130] See in this regard Vec, 'Congress of Vienna', 657.

[131] Ibid., with reference to Constantin Frantz, *Der Föderalismus* (Mainz: F Kirchheim: 1879), 372.

[132] See above text at notes 119 and 120.

many of Krisch's examples? Who preselects the candidates for the position of judges of the European Court of Human Rights? Who are members of the Security Council and who elects them? Who composes the World Trade Organisation Dispute Settlement Body? In all these cases we have to acknowledge the involvement and the determining role of states.

Bourdieu highlights the importance of paying attention to and being able to be surprised by such simple statements as 'He was appointed as professor.'[133] Because only by paying attention to these apparently insignificant details can we stand a chance of overcoming state thinking. Therefore, states remain central actors within this arena that Krisch describes as becoming postnational. However, he and several other commentators are right to highlight that the mechanisms at play and the ways states intervene evolve over time. Perhaps they become subtler. However, this does not justify calling these changes postnational. In doing so we conceal the ways in which states and state thinking still determine our framing of the global. What is needed in this situation is a clearer articulation of these more subtle and less visible ways in which states shape the global today, how they interact with actors that try to contest, resist or escape state authority. The most valuable part of Krisch's contribution is his engagement with some of these issues.

c) Conclusions

By comparing Teubner's work on societal constitutionalism and Krisch's idea of pluralist structure of postnational law, we can notice that, in both cases, state thinking is at play, that state remains the main framing element. This is more obvious and more clearly visible in Teubner's work. His direct recourse to the notion of constitutionalism, although within a framework very different from the mainstream global constitutionalism discourse, leads to his construction taking the shape of a state. In Krisch's postnational law viewed through a pluralist lens, the state becomes almost invisible. However, at a closer reading we can see how state thinking is at play. I would argue that by using the language that conceals the presence of the state, Krisch's thinking contributes to the continuing domination of the state more significantly.

In conclusion, state thinking remains the main frame within which discourses on the structuring of the global operate. This is true of the global constitutionalism and is easier to recognise because a direct

[133] Bourdieu, *Sur l'État*, 431; Bourdieu, *Langage et pouvoir symbolique*, 307–321.

analogy to a typically state-related concept is used. However, this is also visible in other attempts that purport to achieve a break from the state: societal constitutionalism and pluralist postnational law. The problematic aspect of the state as a structuring device relates to the mechanisms inherent in the state form. As discussed at the beginning of this chapter, the aim of global constitutionalism can broadly be defined as promoting a better life for every individual through constraint of arbitrariness. However, the state is based on a mechanism that contains within itself an exclusion/inclusion dynamic that conceals and facilitates some forms of arbitrariness. Similarly to the dominant paradigm of the individual discussed in the previous section, the state as a monopolising and universalising device through the monopolisation of various forms of capital produces a discourse that is easily accepted as universal but is based on suppression and exclusion of alternative visions and ways of life. Therefore, global constitutionalism can never achieve its goals as long as the state remains its structuring device, even if in subtle and less visible ways.

Is it at all possible to avoid state thinking? Is it possible to un-think the state? There is no simple answer to these questions and therefore, a paradigm shift in this area is very difficult to achieve. We will return to this in relation to human rights and global constitutionalism in the coming chapters, but most importantly in the concluding chapter, where a fuller picture provides better basis for formulating some suggestions. At this stage we can recall Bourdieu's reflections on his methodology that paying attention to simple and obvious things, questioning the obviousness of such statements as 'He was appointed judge/or professor', contributes to reveal state's structuring power. Historical enquiry in the form of genetic history is the most important element because it helps revealing that moment in the past when alternatives were eliminated, and as a result, certain ways of thinking and doing became unquestionable truth while others disappeared. Within this study, an exercise in genetic history is attempted in Chapter 3, where ancient Greek and early Islamic traditions are discussed. However, before we go to next chapters, we need to consider the final paradigmatic element of constitutionalism, namely the political.

3 *Politics of International Constitutionalism*

Constitutionalism is traditionally viewed in the legal literature as a normative or more precisely legal concept. Especially, the tradition of international or global constitutionalism is closely tied to the project of juridification of international affairs and the quest for establishing international law as a discipline distinct from international politics. However, the concept of constitutionalism is heavily loaded with political connotations, the best evidence being the debate between proponents of political and legal constitutionalism. Therefore, the little attention devoted to the political within discussions on global constitutionalism is highly problematic. This part's main purpose is to demonstrate inadequacy of theorising international or global constitutionalism without paying due attention to the political. It demonstrates that different visions of the political can lead to contradictory visions of global constitutionalism and its future. It also provides an initial diagnosis of the dominant paradigm of the political in international constitutionalism. Finally, it also suggests a possible way forward in undoing the presently dominant paradigm of the political.

This part starts by depicting the dominance of the legal perspective in the current state of discussions of international constitutionalism. It then goes on to present how some scholars attempted a discussion of political elements. More specifically, the notion of democracy and the active subject of constitutionalism are discussed in more detail. In order to identify the paradigm of the political that dominates these themes in international constitutionalism, two contrasting visions of the political developed by Schmitt and Agamben respectively are presented. The concluding section of this part suggest possible strategies in thinking the political in line with the overall orientation of global constitutionalism.

a) Law over Politics in International Constitutionalism

The very existence of the debate between proponents of political and legal constitutionalism sheds more light on tensions surrounding the issue of the political in global constitutionalism. In a nutshell, legal constitutionalism views bills of rights and judicial review as the best mechanisms to prevent and constrain any arbitrary exercise of power.[134] From the perspective of political constitutionalism, democratic political structures and processes themselves are a sufficient and even a better guarantee of a healthily functioning political system than any bills of rights or courts.[135]

[134] One of the best and most well-known defenders of legal constitutionalism within domestic context is Ronald Dworkin. His most widely known work is Dworkin, *Taking Rights Seriously*.

[135] For a particularly powerful plea see Bellamy, *Political Constitutionalism*. Another author with a strong penchant towards political constitutionalism is Loughlin. However, he often uses more general terms such as 'public law' and 'political jurisprudence'. Nevertheless since the core of his enquiry is how the governmental authority is

Obviously, there will be nuances in how particular authors view either legal or political constitutionalism, and some will take elements of political constitutionalism into their theories of legal constitutionalism and vice versa. However, the heavier reliance on either of the two elements demarcates the two visions of constitutionalism.

Even beyond this division between legal and political constitutionalism, there is a general acknowledgement in the broader literature on constitutionalism that constitutionalism as a concept implies an interweaving between law and politics.[136] It can be described as a simultaneous creation of the possibilities for and limitations upon the exercise of power.[137] The elements that allow the creation of power and limitations upon it can be both legal and political. However, since fundamentally constitutionalism deals with power within communities, it is hard to see how a full understanding of constitutionalism can be achieved without considering the political side. Therefore, one would presume that the literature on global constitutionalism would accord an equal degree of attention to political as well as legal elements of constitutionalisation processes taking place at the global level. Unfortunately, this is not the case. The legal constitutionalist perspective heavily dominates the current literature on global constitutionalism. It is characterised by a very detailed examination of legal or institutional elements at the expense of considering the political to the point that the political seems to disappear from the global constitutionalist discourse.[138] This can be partly explained by international lawyers'

constituted, it is a constitutional enquiry. See e.g. Loughlin, *Idea of Public Law;* or Loughlin, *Foundations of Public Law.*

136 For instance, Loughlin defines this as a tension between the text (a set of rules that establishes and regulates the activity of governing within a state) and the political way of being: Loughlin, 'Constitutional Theory'.

137 For a clear and compelling articulation of this idea see e.g. Scott, '(Political) Constitutions'.

138 Even scholars who write about global constitutionalism from a different disciplinary perspective will still heavily rely on the centrality of normative ordering. See e.g. Kjaer, *Constitutionalism.* For a different example, see Somek, *Cosmopolitan Constitution*: although he talks about the political face of cosmopolitan constitution, this political face is actually reduced to the legal, namely authority as constrained by human rights and principles of non-discrimination (244–283, in particular Chapter 5). It should be noted that what sometimes is called the functionalist approach to global constitutionalism does not engage in the discussion of the political in a sense of political constitutionalism because it also heavily relies on standardised procedures, regulatory agreements and existing institutions, and thus on the already legalised environment. For a general description of functionalist school see Wiener et al., 'Global Constitutionalism', 7.

unstated prejudices against anything political. Traditionally, the discipline of international law has had to defend its identity as a legal discipline separate from politics. This defensive position and ensuing over-emphasis on the legal is still often visible in discourses of international lawyers.

Historically, this situation can be traced back to the effort by Alfred Verdross at building up a science of public international law. In doing so, Alfred Verdross also made one of the first or perhaps even the first systematic attempt to analyse international law through an explicitly constitutional lens.[139] His approach was deeply influenced by Kelsen's pure theory of law and the idea of *Grundnorm*. In the introduction to his second book dealing with international law from a constitutional perspective, Verdross establishes a clear correlation between his work on the topic and Kelsen's concepts. Thus, he clarifies that his first book on the topic published in 1923 and entitled *Einheit des rechtlichen Weltbildes auf Grundlage der Völkerrechtsverfassung* uses the term 'constitution' in the sense of *Grundnorm* ('Verfassung im "rechtslogischen", rechtssystematischen Sinne' as he clarifies it).[140] Whereas his second book, published in 1926 and entitled *Die Verfassung der Völkerrechtsgemeinschaft*, uses the term 'constitution' in the sense of material constitution understanding it as 'jene Normen, die den Aufbau, die Gliederung und die Zuständigkeit einer Gemeinschaft zum Gegenstand haben.'[141] In addition, Verdross' approach, similarly to Kelsen's, is motivated by the desire to establish international law and law more generally as a neutral and objective scientific discipline separate from neighbouring fields such as sociology or politics. This is particularly visible in his multiple references to and comparisons with the scientific methodology in physics or natural science.[142] Within this type of a theoretical framework it becomes difficult to justify any analysis of political elements. If law is simply law, a self-referential isolated discipline, why and how should the political be considered within it?

[139] While some authors used the term 'constitution' in relation to international law as early as the nineteenth century, to my knowledge, these uses of the term did not lead to a systematic reflection upon this topic. None of the earlier authors proposed such a comprehensive and detailed theory of international constitutional law as Verdross. See e.g. the second volume of *Handbuch des Völkerrechts* by Holtzendorff, which is entitled *Die völkerrechtliche Verfassung und Grundordnung der auswärtigen Staatsbeziehungen* (The Constitution of International Law and the Basic Order of External Relations between States). Despite its title, the volume simply provides an overview of the notion of state personality, and the rights and duties of states.

[140] Verdross, *Verfassung*, V. [141] Ibid.

[142] See in particular the introduction to his 1923 book: Verdross, *Einheit des rechtlichen Weltbildes*, V.

The work of Kelsen, and particularly Verdross' extension of Kelsen's thought to public international law, has been highly influential on several generations of international lawyers.[143] In particular, many scholars working on the idea of constitutionalisation of international law stand firmly at a continuum of Verdross' initial discussion of public international law from a constitutionalist perspective.[144] Since a wide range of international law scholars even today follow either consciously or unconsciously the view of international law and consequently of international constitutionalism as advocated and developed by Verdross, the discussion of the political becomes unnecessary or even damaging.

The dominant view of global constitutionalism present in the works of international lawyers highlights such elements of constitutionalism as rule of law and rights protection; they would also mention democracy and separation of powers at times, but would leave to the side the underlying political dynamics and mechanisms.[145] The emphasis on the legal aspects of constitutionalism is partly justified by the nature of the discipline. However, it also obscures and leaves important aspects of constitutionalisation processes uninvestigated, be they real or imagined. In this regard the growing interest of international lawyers in sociological and political theories and the ensuing richer literature informed by other disciplines fills some gaps.

In the remainder of this section the views existing in international constitutionalism on two political elements of global constitutionalism are presented: democracy and the active subject of constitutionalism. These two aspects are chosen because they attracted slightly more attention from scholars. The analysis of the discussion of these two elements is

[143] See e.g. a special section devoted to the international law thought of Alfred Verdross in 1995 in the *European Journal of International Law.*

[144] On this see Kleinlein, 'Alfred Verdross'. Although the title of his article ends with a question mark, the answer provided in the article affirms the influence of Verdross. He highlights nuances of understanding and use of the term constitutionalism, but does not deny the influence exercised by Verdross (see at 416 in particular); and O'Donoghue, 'Alfred Verdross'.

[145] For instance, even when authors discuss separation of powers or democracy as necessary elements of constitutionalism, when depicting these elements in international constitutionalism, they either admit that these elements are not realised at the international level or reduce them to some substitute mechanisms. This later strategy is discussed in relation to democracy in more detail in the next section. For an example of the first strategy in relation of separation of powers see e.g. Paulus, 'International Legal System', 100–101.

presented with the aim of identifying the underlying view of the political in global constitutionalism. This serves as a basis for a further discussion of the paradigm of the political in global constitutionalism.

(1) Considering Democracy One aspect of the political in global constitutionalism that attracted some degree of attention from international law scholars working on the issue of constitutionalisation of international law is democracy deficit in international law. Discussions of this topic are not too numerous, but provide some important insights into the way this strand of international law scholarship approaches some fundamental political aspects of proposed constitutionalisation processes at the global level.[146]

For some scholars the discussion on democracy in global constitutionalism does not need to go beyond the implementation of the right to democracy within states. For example, for De Wet democracy is just one of the values that gains importance for the international community as a whole and thus represents one of the proofs for constitutionalisation of international law.[147] Other scholars criticise excessive reliance on democracy as accountability through the democratic electoral process. For instance, Kumm advocates a broader notion of input legitimacy that takes into account a range of actors involved in decision-making and thus, according to him, leads to an enhanced participation of wider community.[148] These positions that trade off either the possibility of a direct say by all affected individual or the direct involvement of individuals and other actors at the international level can be contrasted with the idea of dual democracy advocated by Peters.[149] Her proposal has double

[146] It is important to highlight that the writings on democracy, and international law more broadly, are more numerous. However, they do not always and systematically connect the issue of democracy in international law to the project of the constitutionalisation of international law. For this reason they are of limited utility for the purposes of our analysis. See e.g. Wheatley, *Democratic Legitimacy*: constitutionalism features as one of the characteristics of international law (Chapter 4) that prepares the ground for a direct discussion of democracy in international law (Chapter 5), but the topics remain otherwise disconnected.

[147] De Wet, 'International Constitutional Order', 63.

[148] Kumm, 'Cosmopolitan Turn', 296. A more detailed articulation of the idea of legitimacy of international law around four principles: legality, subsidiarity, accountability and participation, and reasonable outcomes without the need for democracy, thus implicitly acknowledging that global constitutionalism does not require democracy is contained in Kumm, 'Legitimacy of International Law'. Similarly, Dunoff and Trachtman, 'Functional Approach', 21.

[149] Peters, 'Dual Democracy' in Klabbers, Peters and Ulfstein, *Constitutionalization*, 263–341.

duality: first it suggests that global constitutionalism requires dual democratic mechanisms both within nation-states and 'above' them, namely at various global governance levels. As far as democracy within states is concerned, Peters postulates it as a necessary but insufficient condition of addressing democracy deficit of global governance. Programmatically, she argues for the acknowledgement of the requirement of democracy within states as 'a global constitutional principle'.[150]

When it comes to addressing democracy deficits 'above' states, Peters suggests two tracks of democratisation: statist and individualist. The statist track 'above' states does not replicate the previously discussed requirement of democratisation within states. Although discussed by Peters quite briefly, the importance of equal participation of states in international institutions and accountability of these institutions to states is highlighted. Thus, she signals out as problematic such persistent situations as the absence of formal equality of states (e.g. existence of permanent members of the Security Council),[151] substantive inequality between states,[152] or weak democratic foundation of foreign politics.[153] The major part of her chapter is dedicated to discussing the second track focused on individuals. This is justified by the fact that 'inter-state paradigm alone cannot lead to a democracy whose ultimate unit of concern are citizens.'[154] In this particular regard, Peters' contribution is very interesting and goes beyond traditional concerns of international lawyers.[155] Her proposals are ultimately very practice-oriented, keeping the existing institutional structures of global governance in mind. They are developed along three lines: global citizenship, participation of civil society actors and institutional design for non-state democratisation. The most interesting part relates to the concrete proposals for transforming existing global governance institutions in a way allowing for direct participation from individuals. The main mechanisms proposed are various forms of transnational referenda and consultations as well as parliamentary assemblies.[156]

Peters acknowledges the tensions and difficulties inherent in her proposal both with regard to the individualist track itself[157] and with regard

[150] Ibid., 264. [151] Ibid., 286–288. [152] Ibid., 190–196. [153] Ibid., 291.
[154] Ibid., 286.
[155] The majority of international law scholars would regard the proposals by Peters as 'impractical' but also as 'not required from the point of view of constitutional theory': Fassbender, 'We the People', 288. Similarly Kumm, 'Legitimacy of International Law', 926; Besson, 'Whose Constitution(s)'.
[156] Peters, 'Dual Democracy', 318–327. [157] Ibid., 330–332.

to the coexistence of two tracks.[158] This leads her to discuss a number of complementary mechanisms of legitimacy and accountability, similarly to several other international constitutionalist scholars. Such elements as inclusion and participation of civil society actors and businesses, expertise, independence of political actors, output legitimacy, strengthening of judicial review, and direct effect of international treaties are highlighted.[159] However, again contrary to many scholars writing on global constitutionalism, Peters suggests that these mechanisms might provide a partial equivalent to democracy 'as long as an elected law-making body is out of sight'.[160] Peters concludes as follows:

> [N]one of the suggested alternative mechanisms of accountability in global governance can in themselves be considered 'democratic'. At best, a combined formula of the procedures and mechanisms discussed ... which would be in themselves normatively deficient might create an overall accountability which is functionally equivalent to democratic deliberation, consultation, votes and elections.[161]

Thus, Peters' distinct contribution consists of the emphasis on the direct input by individuals as the only truly democratic process. Recognition of difficulties that the implementation of this vision of democracy at the international level presents, leads to the acceptance of other forms of democratic legitimacy as a short-term solution, but not as a definite trade-off.

This analysis of democracy is centred around issues of institutional design and structures. Therefore, it represents one of the rare attempts by international lawyers to address directly the criticism of democratic deficiency of structures and institutions of international law without turning to substitutes. However, although it opens up a space for input from individuals, states firmly remain basic structuring units. For individuals to be able to participate in parliamentary assemblies or referenda, they need to be citizens of some states or be lawful residents. Within this scheme the situation of migrants, asylum seekers and some other marginalised groups remains unresolved. Potentially, functional or affectedness-based selection of populations mentioned by Peters could offer an avenue for overcoming this hurdle. However, Peters herself dismissed it as unrealistic for the moment. Therefore, one of the most difficult conundrums of the current human rights and broader international law regime, namely the place and status of undocumented migrants, refugees and stateless persons highlighted before, remains unresolved.[162] Similarly, as

[158] Ibid., 333–338. [159] Ibid., 338–341. [160] Ibid., 338. [161] Ibid., 341.
[162] See in particular section 'Individuals within Global Constitutionalism' above.

long as there is no move away from statist to functional models of consultation of individuals, mechanisms of representation will remain controlled by states, thus keeping existing inequalities and biases in place. However, these debates on the place of democracy in global constitutionalism and especially the difficulty international law scholars have with accepting the direct involvement of individuals in decisions at the international level leads to a more fundamental political question of constitutionalism, namely that of the active subject of constitutionalism.

(2) The Active Subject and the Political Who is included in democracy? Who is that subject whose opinion counts? In terms of the national constitutional tradition around which constitutional theory and various discussions about the relationship between democracy and constitutionalism evolve, the answer is quite simple: the citizens of a particular state. However, when we think about international law, the answer becomes more confusing and less obvious. As mentioned above, from the perspective of global constitutionalism, the individual is positioned at the centre of preoccupations. Logically, from this central position of the individual, the affirmation that each and every individual constitutes the active subject of international constitutionalism should follow. This is, however, far from straightforward. We have already seen in the previous section, how challenging are the attempts at founding democracy in global constitutionalism on the direct involvement of affected individuals. Thus, within the broad context of international constitutionalism, 'Hitherto the debate has not engaged with the identification of a constitutional constituency, disregarding the key issues of whom such a process addresses and who gains from constitutional purchase.'[163] One possible starting point for reflecting on this issue is provided by the notion of constituency as articulated by O'Donoghue. In this view constituency is set in opposition to the notion of community, which is too vague and loaded with values and interests.[164] In order to fully grasp the contours of constituency, one needs to decide 'who may rightfully exercise constituent power within a democratically legitimate process'.[165]

Thus, constituency is described as being situated 'in the nexus between constituted and constituent power, or as the space where power is exercised and vested outside of a distinct group but on their behalf and in their interest, the assemblage may be described as a constituency.'[166]

[163] O'Donoghue, *Constitutionalism*, 247. [164] Ibid., 240. [165] Ibid., 240.
[166] Ibid., 236.

O'Donoghue emphasises two important aspects of constituency: its procedural character[167] and its link to law.[168] In relation to the constituency in international law, O'Donoghue makes one important remark: 'Identifying the process in global law required for constituency to emerge is difficult.'[169] Therefore, while a way towards a better grappling with the active subject of international constitutionalism is opened, it remains tied to law and burdened by practical difficulties.

The above discussion indicates that state paradigm or the state as the structuring device of our thinking prevents a renewal in the international law scholarship dealing with the global because of the dominance of the legal component that itself is too strongly tied to the development of the state form in the Western tradition. The link to the state through the existing international institutions and mechanisms is also clearly visible in the preceding discussion of democracy in international constitutionalism. However, the state is as much a legal as it is a political entity, so perhaps thinking the political differently, beyond the Western philosophical tradition, could be the most productive way to break the circle within which the scholarship on international constitutionalism remains caught. The next section demonstrates that any vision of international or global constitutionalism, even if it is based on legal or normative notions, has an underlying vision of the political. Depending on the underlying vision of the political, the possibilities of theorising global constitutionalism will be more or less limited. I will argue that the dominant vision of the political tied to Western experience with law and the state form is antithetical to global constitutionalism's goals. In order to overcome these limitations, scholars need to articulate clearly their vision of the political and reformulate it if necessary. In order to defend this argument, the next section discusses two contrasting visions of the political and their respective consequences for the possibility of global constitutionalism: one articulated by Carl Schmitt and another one developed by Giorgio Agamben. The main reason for selecting these two authors is the opposing consequences of their visions of the political for the possibility of global constitutionalism that well illustrate the argument.

(a) Schmitt: Friend and Enemy

Carl Schmitt's is one of the best-known attempts at providing a general definition of the political 'by discovering and defining the specifically political categories'.[170] When Schmitt attempts to define the political he

[167] Ibid., 225, 238–240. [168] Ibid., 238–239. [169] Ibid., 239.
[170] Schmitt, *Concept*, 25.

adopts a particular approach to definition. He recognises that the state and the political are often brought together and even equated to each other, but affirms that this way of defining the political is unhelpful, especially because the state today is not 'a truly clear and unequivocal eminent entity confronting non-political groups and affairs'.[171] Therefore, he affirms that a definition of the political is only possible through identification of the specifically political categories.[172] These specifically political couple of categories are, according to Schmitt, friend and enemy.

Schmitt explains in detail what he means by enemy and how an enemy in a political sense is different from an enemy in other contexts. In order to fully understand Schmitt's conception of the political, it is important to keep in mind the specificities of his own definition of an enemy. Schmitt carefully distinguishes an enemy in the political sense from a competitor, an adversary or a private enemy. One of the central sentences that summarises the essence of Schmitt's understanding of a political enemy is the following: 'Feind ist nur eine wenigstens eventuell, d.h. der realen Möglichkeit nach kämpfende Gesamtheit von Menschen, die einer ebensolchen Gesamtheit gegenübersteht.'[173] In the English translation used here, this sentence reads as follows: 'An enemy exist only when, at least potentially, one fighting collectivity of people confronts a similar collectivity.'[174] The German original text is important for the purposes of the argument as developed here. Schmitt emphasises from the outset that 'the friend and enemy concepts are to be understood in their concrete and existential sense, not as metaphors or symbols'.[175] In this regard he also clarifies the meaning of '*kämpfende*' and '*Kampf*', which in English are translated using two terms with different roots: fighting and combat. In this translation the intimate relationship between the definition of the enemy and the combat (Kampf, kämpfende) can be easily lost.

> Ebenso wie das Wort Feind, ist hier das Wort Kampf im Sinne einer seinsmäßigen Ursprünglichkeit zu verstehen. Es bedeutet nicht Konkurrenz, nicht den "rein geistigen" Kampf der Discussion, nicht das symbolische "Ringen" . . . Die Begriffe Freund, Feind und Kampf erhalten ihren Sinn dadurch, Dass sie insbesondere auf *die reale Möglichkeit der physischen Tötung* Bezug haben und behalten.[176]

In the English translation, this last sentence reads as follows: 'The friend, enemy, and combat concepts receive their real meaning precisely because

[171] Ibid., 22. [172] Ibid., 25. [173] Schmitt, *Begriff*, 29. [174] Schmitt, *Concept*, 29.
[175] Ibid., 27. [176] Schmitt, *Begriff*, 33, emphasis added.

they refer to *the real possibility of physical killing*.'[177] This means that the real possibility of one group of people uniting to physically kill another group of human beings is what defines the political for Schmitt.

The importance of emphasising these aspects of Schmitt's definition of enemy and fight or combat is that a particular vision of the political arises from these characteristics. For instance some thinkers attempted to use Schmitt's idea of the political to construct a different vision of the political within a constitutionalist framework. However, in doing so they use the terms 'enemy' and 'combat' in a symbolic, figurative sense that goes against Schmitt's own articulation of the political.

Another important aspect of Schmitt's definition of the political is his emphasis on potentiality as a real possibility of something: conflict, war or existence of the enemy. For example, in both quotations above, Schmitt does not posit the confrontation between fighting collectivities as necessarily taking place now, as an actualisation of this fighting, but only as a potentiality, a possibility that nevertheless needs to be real ('der realen Möglichkeit nach' in the first German quotation is lost in the English translation). Similarly, when defining the combat (Kampf) Schmitt does not require the actuality of the physical killing but only its *possibility, real* possibility. The same aspect is emphasised when Schmitt discusses war as an extreme consequence of enmity and as a specifically political behaviour. Schmitt insists that war does not need to be 'common, normal, something ideal, or desirable'.[178] However, the *real possibility* of war is a determining characteristic of the specifically political behaviour.[179]

In the Schmittean vision, a community defines itself through the determinations made about this community's friend and enemy. The emphasis is placed on this group inside/outside dynamic that is determined by the possibility of war, destruction and death. Fearing death, human beings unite themselves in order to protect themselves from human beings that are defined as enemies. Thus, the existence of a community and for the purposes of Schmitt's definition of a very specific type of community exemplified by the state form is central to the possibility of politics and the political. The unity of the community emerges only because there is a fear and division among human beings. In this

[177] Schmitt, *Concept*, 33, emphasis added. [178] Ibid.

[179] More specifically, he states, 'War is neither the aim nor the purpose nor even the very content of politics. But as an ever present possibility it is the leading presupposition which determines in a characteristic way human action and thinking and thereby creates a specifically political behavior.' Ibid., 34. See also 33, 35.

definition of the political, strong parallels to the mechanics of exclusion/inclusion highlighted above in relation to the contemporary paradigm of the individual as a right-bearer as well as in relation to the state are visible. We will see that for Agamben the notion of community is also central for his definition of the coming politics. However, the community Agamben postulates as central to his politics is radically different from the Schmittean political community.

(b) Agamben: Whatever Singularity and Belonging

Giorgio Agamben develops a contrasting vision of the political. It should be clarified that this contrasting vision of the political does not emerge directly from his writings on *homo sacer* that represent more or less the diagnosis of modern and contemporary politics,[180] but from his more marginal (in terms of the depth and breadth of their elaboration) and less well-known thoughts on the radically new or coming politics and the coming community.[181]

One fundamental feature of the coming politics and the associated life 'that are yet to be entirely thought' according to Agamben is their non-statal and non-juridical character.[182] First, it is significant that even if Agamben speaks of the 'non-statal' he does not only speak of a 'non-statal life' that we could perhaps start imagining easier, but also of 'non-statal politics', which is more paradoxical. For instance, Schmitt and scholars subscribing to his vision of the political cannot imagine politics without states or state-like structures. However, Agamben thinks that the political can and the new politics should exist beyond and without states. Moreover, his vision of new politics calls for the disappearance of states. In this context, what justifies Agamben's claim that politics can be non-statal? If Agamben keeps the term 'political' in this context, it means that something fundamental about politics will remain even in this non-statal and non-juridical environment. An important hint towards this new politics is provided in the following sentence:

180 This series is most well known for its two earlier volumes: *Homo Sacer* and *State of Exception*. Other volumes that have relevance to some of the ideas related to the notion of the political are less widely known. The last volume in this series was published in an English translation in 2016: Agamben, *Use of Bodies* and contains some developments relevant for this book.

181 Although it should be emphasised that his whole series on *homo sacer* to a significant extent can be read as a ground-clearing and preparation of his proposal on coming politics that to some extent appears in the last volume.

182 Agamben, *Means*, 112.

> If there is today a social power [potenza], it must see its own impotence [impotenza] through to the end, it must decline any will to either posit or preserve right, it must break everywhere the nexus between violence and rights, between the living and language that constitutes sovereignty.[183]

Agamben points here to the necessity of breaking up traditional connections that constitute modern visions of the political, including the notion of sovereignty and law that proceeds through the use of violence to impose right.

However, a series of questions arise for many contemporary thinkers. One fundamental question is well formulated by Derrida in different places but can be summarised as follows: can we abandon the notions of sovereignty, state and law without abandoning the idea of liberty, freedom or human rights? As Derrida says, 'one cannot combat, *head-on, all* sovereignty *in general*, without threatening at the same time, beyond the nation-state figure of sovereignty, the classical principles of freedom and self-determination'.[184] More broadly, is it possible to think a non-statal and non-juridical world where human beings will live a happy life?[185] Is it possible to pursue political life and social struggles without claiming any rights? Derrida, despite his acute awareness of this difficulty and apparent contradiction does not deny the possibility of thinking anew such notions as sovereignty, liberty, states or rights. For instance in his seminar *The Beast and the Sovereign*, he affirms his desire to deconstruct the dominant logic and concept of nation state sovereignty without arriving at depoliticisation but at a re-politicisation that avoids the pitfalls that he criticises in the dominant vision of sovereignty.[186] Therefore, it is conceivable to take Agamben's thoughts on coming politics seriously despite all the paradoxes they entail.

So what does this coming politics mean and how can it take shape? Agamben states that

> The novelty of the coming politics is that it will not longer be a struggle for the conquest or control of the State, but a struggle between the State and the non-State (humanity), an insurmountable disjunction between whatever singularity and the State organization.[187]

[183] Ibid., 113. [184] Derrida, *Rogues*, 158.

[185] 'Happy life' is how Agamben defines the goal or the ultimate outcome of the coming politics. Agamben, *Means*, 114–115 in particular: 'This "happy life" should be, rather, an absolutely profane "sufficient life" that has reached the perfection of its own power and of its own communicability – a life over which sovereignty and right no longer have any hold.'

[186] Derrida, *Séminaire*, 112. [187] Agamben, *Coming*, 85.

There are two important terms appearing in this quotation to which we will devote more attention. These terms are: 'whatever singularity' and 'humanity' as the non-state. Whatever singularity is defined in the same essay as 'a being whose community is mediated not by any condition of belonging . . . nor by the simple absence of conditions . . . but by belonging itself'.[188] What is interesting in this statement is the maintenance of the notion of community that is central to the definition of the political, to the very possibility of the political. However, as Agamben emphasises, this is a very different community from the one familiar to us, because whatever singularities that compose this community are not united by any identity. Thus, in order to be formed this community does not need the friend-enemy distinction, even in a symbolic form. It is a 'co-belonging without any representable condition of belonging'.[189] This type of belonging is possible only for whatever singularities. The 'whatever' does not mean 'being it does not matter which' but 'being such as that it always matters'.[190] The singularity is better understood through Agamben's discussion of the relationship between the common and the singular. The singularity in the way Agamben presents it is 'absolutely inessential'.[191] Therefore, the commonality that he emphasises is also an inessential commonality. This commonality is closely tied to the notion of the common that Agamben defines as 'a point of indifference between the proper and the improper' that can be grasped only as use.[192] Agamben suggests that 'the essential political problem then becomes: "How does one use a *common*?"'[193] Agamben indicates the experience of thought as being 'always an experience of a potential and of a common use'.[194] It is clear that within this vision of the political, the need for law and division disappears: since community is defined by the belonging itself, by the use of a common, there is no need for states as separate and potentially hostile entities.

As far as humanity is concerned, I highlight the opposition in which it is placed against the state; it confronts the state without wanting to become a new state or to control an existing state. Therefore, this humanity is opposed to the state logic. Its common action – and therefore political action – is not directed against any state in particular but against the very essence of the statal logic with the aim of depositing it completely. While for Schmitt, humanity is an ideological construct misused for political

[188] Ibid. [189] Ibid., 86. [190] Ibid., 2. [191] Ibid., 18.

[192] Agamben, *Means*, 117. The notion of 'use' features prominently in two volumes of the *homo sacer* series: Agamben, *Highest Poverty* and Agamben, *Use*.

[193] Agamben, *Means*, 117, emphasis in the original. [194] Agamben, *Use*, 211.

purposes,[195] for Agamben the notion of humanity becomes the subject that has the capacity to create new politics by depositing the state logic. Agamben defines humanity through the notion of whatever singularity connecting both through thought. Thought, and more specifically the potential of thought, is a generic potential of humanity constituting it as a multitude.[196]

In order to further develop and illustrate the vision of coming politics, I will use an example that highlights several aspects of the coming politics as they emerge from community defined by whatever singularity. In my interpretation of this vision of politics – Agamben's coming politics – the central figure that exemplifies several of the above characteristics of the coming politics is the figure of Bartleby. This example will also help us understand the difference between Schmitt's and Agamben's references to potentiality.

Bartleby is a protagonist in Herman Melville's short story 'Bartleby, the Scrivener: A Story of Wall Street'. In this story, Bartleby was a clerk with the main responsibility of copying and proofreading texts. One day he stops this activity, pronouncing the sentence around which many philosophical reflections, including Agamben's, revolve: 'I would prefer not to'. This utterance is neither an affirmation nor a negation. It is characterised as 'agrammatical'[197] and analysed by Agamben within the context of the issue of potentiality. Potentiality is not only potentiality to be, but, what Agamben emphasises strongly, potentiality to *not* be. These two modes of potentiality do not stand in symmetry because potentiality to be has as its object a certain act, whereas the potentiality to not be has as its object potentiality itself.[198] Our inability today to fully think the potentiality can be linked to what Agamben describes as the reduction of potentiality to the terms of will and necessity,[199] whereas Bartleby 'succeeds in being able (and not being able) absolutely without wanting it'.[200] It is important to emphasise that Bartleby never completes the utterance 'I would prefer not to'. He does not say 'I would prefer not to do so and so' but simply 'I would prefer not to'. He also does not say 'I prefer not to' – this would be an expression of preference and therefore some form of will – but 'I would prefer not to'. And thus the only possible meaning of human freedom is expressed, according to Agamben, in the following formula by Duns Scotus: 'he who wills experiences the capacity

[195] See e.g. Schmitt, *Concept*, 54. [196] Agamben, *Use*, 213. [197] Deleuze, 'Bartleby', 68.
[198] Agamben, *Coming*, 34–35. [199] Agamben, 'Bartleby', 254. [200] Ibid., 255.

not to will' (*experitur qui vult se posse non velle*).[201] The importance of this figure and associated notions to Agamben's coming politics becomes particularly clear when Agamben affirms that '[o]nly power that is capable of both power and impotence, then, is the supreme power.'[202] This connects us back to the one of Agamben's quotations where he emphasises the need today for a power that recognises and lives through its own impotence. The power is thus redefined in a radical way that also helps us to think differently about politics and the subject of these politics.

The notion of potentiality is very important to Agamben's and Schmitt's definition of politics. However, for Schmitt the potentiality is a real possibility of something, especially of a violent act that can produce death as a consequence. Agamben rediscovers potentiality in a completely different form. We would say that this potentiality is passive, but this would not do justice to the richness of this potentiality to not be. Within the context of this potentiality to not be, the idea of political action acquires a completely new sense that goes beyond claiming rights. Potentiality to not be and pure mediality of politics[203] realises its power in a negative sense as a power to be affected, as a power to be united by the very condition of belonging. This thought, according to Agamben, 'must become the guiding concept and the unitary centre of coming politics':[204] it 'does not mean simply being affected by this or that thing (. . .), but being at the same time affected by one's own receptivity, gaining experience, in every thought, of a pure potential of thought.'[205] This inessential commonality that does not need a state or identity or a characteristic according to which belonging is defined can encompass the whole of humanity without any difficulty. Politics redefined on the basis of the pure mediality of the power to be affected by own's one receptivity open up a new horizon for imagining the global ordering. In the next section we will take a closer look at the consequences of these two contrasting visions of the political for the project of global constitutionalism.

201 Ibid., 262. The Latin phrase is as it appears in Agamben. The full sentence as contained in Duns Scotus' work reads as follows: 'Experitur enim qui vult se posse non velle sive nolle, iuxta quod de libertate voluntaris alibi diffusius habetur.' Duns Scoti, *Quaestiones*, IX, q. 15, 609–610.

202 Agamben, *Coming*, 36.

203 Agamben also identifies pure mediality as an essential characteristic of politics: 'Politics is the sphere neither of an end in itself nor of means subordinated to an end; rather, it is the sphere of a pure mediality without end intended as the field of human action and of human thought.' Agamben, *Means*, 116–117.

204 Agamben, *Use*, 213. 205 Agamben, *Use*, 211.

(c) Prospects of Global Constitutionalism in Light of Visions of the Political

These two contrasting visions of the political lead to opposite conclusions as far as the possibility of global constitutionalism is concerned. Obviously, there exists an array of different visions of global constitutionalism. The opponents of global constitutionalism also differ, with some still admitting a possibility of some sort of global ordering and others denying it. Nevertheless, whatever the form global constitutionalism takes, it will be impossible without a global community or another form of global active subject. As was demonstrated above, for both authors, a community – although understood differently by them – is a necessary precondition of the political.

With regard to the possibility of some form of global community or organisation, Agamben and Schmitt express opposing views that are tied to their respective visions of the political. According to Schmitt 'global organization means nothing else than the utopian idea of total depolitization'.[206] For Schmitt, the concepts of humanity and universality are not political concepts. They are, according to him, ideological constructs that are misused for political purposes. He especially emphasises that 'wars waged in the name of humanity' have 'an especially intensive political meaning'.[207] He also states, 'Universality at any price would necessarily have to mean total depolitisation and with it, particularly, the nonexistence of states.'[208] Therefore, somebody subscribing to Schmitt's views would never call for the disappearance of states. And inversely, somebody insisting on the impossibility of thinking about politics beyond and without states should be aware of the possible Schmittean consequences of this position. In particular, for Schmitt there is no politics if there are no states, no outside/inside (exclusion/inclusion) dynamic, and no possibility of distinguishing friend from enemy, no real possibility of killing. Even if existing in a modified form, with fewer powers, with divided sovereignty, states remain a necessary precondition according to Schmitt of any political existence. The state is a central pacifying unit of Schmitt's vision of the political. It is able to achieve the pacification and unification only because it defines itself as distinct from enemies that are externalised. We should

[206] Schmitt, *Concept*, 55. The full sentence in German reads as follows: 'Außerdem aber konnte die Gründung eines die ganze Menschheit umfassenden Völkerbundes endlich auch der bisher freilich nur sehr unklaren Tendenz entsprechen, einen unpolitischen Idealzustand des Universal-Gesellschaft "Menschheit" zu organisieren.' Schmitt, *Begriff*, 56.

[207] Schmitt, *Concept*, 54. [208] Ibid., 55.

also remember that for Schmitt the political appears when one group of people that needs to be relatively homogenous, opposes another homogeneous group of people with the real possibility of killing if needed in order to defend its unity and homogeneity. Also, for Schmitt the decision about the friend-enemy distinction and what to do if the unity (state) is threatened is a political decision that cannot be left to law. Therefore, global constitutionalism as a regulation of conduct by states, constraining their discretionary power is impossible for Schmitt. More seriously, he would accuse proponents of global constitutionalism of ideological manipulation for political purposes. Equally impossible for Schmitt is global constitutionalism that overcomes states because then there are no politics, only ideological misuse.

Agamben's vision of politics allows envisaging a global community. Moreover, the community is global in an immediate sense not mediated by states. Schmitt's vision of the political so closely linked to the state form reminds us that whenever the state form is maintained, the friend-enemy distinction and thus the exclusion/inclusion dynamic highlighted in previous parts will reappear sooner or later. With regard to aspirations of scholars working in the field of global constitutionalism, this debate between Schmitt and Agamben is of fundamental significance. The contrast between the opinions of Schmitt and Agamben leads to a new perspective on the notion of the political and its significance for global constitutionalism. In particular, if we ask what justifies the maintenance of the term 'political' for Agamben as compared to Schmitt, the collective dimension will emerge as a common element. However, Schmitt and Agamben will present radically different views of this collective. Although Schmitt and Agamben converge in the fact that the collective that the political life presupposes is needed to enhance the well-being of the members of the collective, they fundamentally disagree on the possibility of envisaging a global political collective. Agamben's view of the collective as composed of whatever singularities united by the belonging itself opens up new directions for thinking the political at the global level. However, this thinking will necessarily need to overcome the statist framework. It is particularly challenging to think about a *global* community. However, community is a necessary precondition of the political, and thus also constitutional ordering. The divergent views on the political offered by Agamben and Schmitt and their consequences highlight the need for scholars working on global constitutionalism to seriously consider the political element of constitutionalism. If global constitutionalism's ultimate aspiration is the well-being of humans – and this transpires in writings of many authors – then perhaps maintaining states, even if just as an actor among others, is fundamentally against constitutionalist aspirations because without rethinking the state we cannot avoid fundamental structures based on outside/inside, exclusion/inclusion. This ultimately maintains the exploitation and suffering of some for the benefit of others, which always implies a real possibility of killing.

This is a very challenging task, and many would question whether such an endeavour of thinking about ordering at the global level without states and without creating a super-state that would promote the well-being of humans can at all be named constitutionalism or be undertaken in the name of constitutionalism. It seems that the ultimate goal of scholars working on global constitutionalism is very similar to the goal of Agamben's coming politics: a happy life for all human beings. Therefore, it is justified to keep the term 'constitutionalism'. However, the very structure within which contemporary discourse on global constitutionalism operates is Schmittean. From the perspective of the Schmittean definition of the political, global constitutionalism's ideals and aspirations are nothing more than empty idealism and perhaps even a disguised political manipulation. Without rethinking the notion of the political and the associated idea of the collective active subject, global constitutionalism will remain a contradiction in terms. Therefore, in order to envisage the future of global ordering that might be able to escape the Schmittean dynamic, global constitutionalism needs to consider the outlines of Agamben's coming politics, envisaging a non-statal and non-juridical ordering of the global. The next few paragraphs will provide a more detailed outline of Agamben's ideas from the perspective of the future of global constitutionalism.

The notion at the heart of the political is the notion of community or, more precisely, the active subject of ordering, in our case global constitutional ordering. The political is fundamentally about ways of constructing the 'we' from a multiplicity of 'I's'. Traditionally, very much in line with Schmittean thinking, all communities define themselves in opposition to something that is outside: by drawing a line, by articulating a difference between 'us' and 'them', between outside and inside. From this perspective, it would seem that thinking about a global community in the way global constitutionalism envisages would be a contradiction in terms. If difference and inside/outside dynamics are essential elements of a community, then we cannot have one single global community. If any type of coming together at the global level can be envisaged, it will always be in a form of a multiplicity of communities either in a state form or in the form of sectorial, interest-related groups in line with societal constitutionalism's claim. From the perspective of the future of the global constitutionalist project we need to ask whether it is possible to think of a community in a different way – escaping the outside/inside dynamic and envisaging a common project and a life together of a multiplicity without unity that needs to distinguish itself from something. Fundamentally, this is what Negri attempted to articulate, whether successfully or not,[209] in his discussion on constituent power, or what Nancy indicated with the notion of 'community without community'.[210] It also seems that Agamben very clearly indicated this possibility in his thoughts on the coming politics and the coming community.[211]

Through the prism of Agamben's philosophy the community that is able to include the whole of humanity needs to be conceived essentially through its belonging and potentiality, but this potentiality is radically different from Schmitt's real possibility. The democratic element of this common being is not the will and preference expressed through voting and representation but the 'whatever' attribute of singularities composing the community: 'being as it always matters' is the essential element of this commonality that is beyond will and necessity. Being beyond will and necessity does not mean passive being; it is simply a different being that overcomes the simple oppositional logic between active and passive modes. Moreover, the whatever singularity as 'being as it always matters' annihilates the need to consider the question of the relationship between constitutionalism and democracy. Since, by definition, being is such as it always matters, there is no need to envisage the formalism of the rights protection, separation of powers and rule of law. Simultaneously, as highlighted above, this same element ensures what traditionally was the task for democracy, namely the relevance of individual opinions, differences, deliberation and so on. The political power is the power to be affected, not the power to act upon others and affect them, even with the loftiest of intentions.

[209] See Negri, *Insurgencies*. For criticism of Negri's position see e.g. Lindahl, 'Paradox of Constituent Power', 501–502 in particular.

[210] This notion was discussed in the section 'From Active Inclusion to Confrontation of Modalities of Exclusion'.

[211] Agamben also uses the term multitude as a political concept central to his idea of coming politics (Agamben, *Use*, 21–213). Although his articulation of multitude differs from the one proposed by Negri, both articulations point towards the possibility of envisaging global community beyond the exclusion/inclusion dynamic.

b) Conclusions

Global constitutionalism tends to postulate the constitutional character of the global ordering based on legal and normative elements such as rights and values. Although some authors expressed concerns at the contradiction between this stance of global constitutionalism and the 'absence of any political authority (or sovereignty or constitution) possessing comparable global and transnational scope',[212] a detailed and deep analysis of the political in global constitutionalism is still lacking. The above discussion demonstrates that this situation can be partly explained by the long-standing tradition of artificially separating the legal and the political in debates on global constitutionalism. Partly, the tension and its intensity depend on the underlying, unstated and often subconscious understanding of the political. It seems that the majority of scholars writing on global constitutionalism hold a vision of the political that is antithetical to the very idea of global constitutionalism, namely the Schmittean vision of the political. Therefore, the first step should be an open and detailed examination of the political components of global constitutionalism and their various understandings alongside its legal elements. Within this context we need also to realise that there are conflicting conceptions of the political, and by privileging one or another we predetermine future developments and foreclose many possibilities that might come with a different vision of the political. In particular, considering the active subject and community with its grounding in democracy in global constitutionalism is absolutely essential.

The hidden or subconscious nature of the political, mostly based on Schmitt's tradition, indicates that perhaps here we have to face one of the moments in the genealogy of global constitutionalism when the phenomenon splits into conscious and unconscious, when one of its founding binary oppositions were produced. This point indicates that for global constitutionalism to affirm itself as an intellectual movement, it needed to hide the fundamental contradiction between the prevalent vision of the political to which it could not yet find any alternative and the aims it pursued. This was done by supressing the political in the discourse of global constitutionalism and by allowing it to appear only as institutionalised or legalised phenomenon. In order to overcome this hurdle and move the project of global constitutionalism further, it is necessary not only to bring the political to consciousness but also to devise strategies for

[212] See e.g. Carrozza, 'Constitutionalism's Post-Modern Opening', 183; or Thornhill, 'Rights and Constituent Power' in general and 385 in particular.

overcoming the Schmittean paradigm that currently permeates our thinking of the political. While paradigms of the individual or the state could remain visible in global constitutionalism because it was possible to present them as compliant with global constitutionalism's goals through an overemphasis on inclusion and relegation of exclusion to the subconscious, the Schmittean political so obviously revealing its nature as antithetical to global constitutionalism needed to be supressed as such. This is a more challenging task, but first steps towards this goal could take the shape of direct consultation of affected individuals or take the form of direct involvement of individuals with implementation of international obligations, as in the example of the private sponsorship of refugees. These practices create space within which divisions and exclusions, and thus the Schmittean vision of the political and community can be overcome. Finally, it is important to highlight how in this discussion of the political, the three paradigms discussed in this chapter come together in an interdependent relationship.

C Distilling Paradigms

This chapter focused on three fundamental paradigms of global constitutionalism: the paradigm of the individual as the point of equilibrium around which everything else is structured, but which remains itself instrumentalised; the paradigm of the state as a structuring device or to use the image of mechanics as gears without which the whole machine stops functioning; and finally the paradigm of the political as a subconscious of global constitutionalism. The political reappears at times in institutionalised or legalised forms, but its subconscious nature points towards the founding event of global constitutionalism that conceals the contradiction inherent in its espousing the dominant vision of the political.

With regard to each paradigm, the chapter demonstrated the discrepancy persisting between the articulated place of each paradigm and the reality of its operation within the tradition of global constitutionalism. Thus, the individual is postulated as the central active subject of global constitutionalism for whom and with whom global constitutionalism exists. However, it operates as a mere object, positioned at the centre but virtually unable to influence what is happening to him or her. The state is presented as one of the many actors that is losing more and more power, and according to some authors it can even be shifted outside of constitutionalism's frame of reference in a sense that constitutionalism can exist without the state. However, the analysis above demonstrated that so far the state operates as the structuring device of global constitutionalism, sometimes more openly through its decisions and sanctioning power, but more often at a less visible cognitive level structuring all possible alternatives. Finally, the political appears in discourse of global constitutionalism only obliquely in certain institutionalised or legalised forms, such as institutionalised democracy or replacement of democracy by 'democratic' normative principles. However, it was demonstrated that the very absence of a direct engagement with the notion of the political exposes the operation of the political at the subconscious level necessary to hide the contradiction between the widely dominant vision of the political (most clearly articulated by Schmitt) and the goals of global constitutionalism. In each case the discrepancy reveals the fundamental paradox at the heart of global constitutionalism, namely that between its stated aim and the mechanisms each paradigm uses. While global constitutionalism attempts to overcome the arbitrariness of power exercised at the global level, it makes use of mechanisms that are built on arbitrariness in the form of exclusion/inclusion. These mechanisms are only apparently geared towards equality and justice. In reality their very operation presupposes some degree of arbitrariness and injustice that these mechanisms use and conceal. The exclusion/inclusion dynamic emerges as a common theme.

The chapter also suggested for each paradigm a way forward into the direction of overcoming or bridging the discrepancy: how an individual can become truly relevant at the international level, how to escape states structuring power and how to bring the political out of the subconscious without destroying the goal that global constitutionalism pursues. In the case of the individual it was suggested that there is a need to find ways to involve individuals directly as makers of practices taking place at the international level to open up space for a direct confrontation of modalities of exclusion. Using the example of the Canadian private sponsorship of refugees programme, the chapter pointed out how this movement could be envisaged in practice. With regard to the structuring power of the state, Bourdieu's work on state thinking was used as an initial indicator of strategies. Based on his methodology it was suggested that questioning small things we take for granted, such as appointments to different international institutions or granting of qualifications combined with an exercise in genetic history, provides the means for overcoming the structuring power of the state. Finally, as far as the political is concerned, there is a need for an explicit examination of the unstated assumptions about the nature of the political, as well as for an explicit articulation of the alternative visions of the political. One such alternative vision of the political that allows pursuing the broad constitutionalist goal understood as happiness for each human being within a community, a concept found in the works of Agamben, was presented. It was also suggested that some practices, such as direct involvement of individuals in law-making or law enforcement, can open up a possibility of overcoming the dominant vision of the political based on exclusion/inclusion and moving towards Agamben's coming community.

In all these cases the challenges of overcoming the discrepancy are huge. However, as the next chapter will demonstrate, the role human rights play in maintaining these discrepancies is fundamental. It will be demonstrated that the operation of the human rights system is essential in keeping the three paradigms discussed in this chapter together. By keeping these paradigms together, human rights reinforce the discrepancies existing between the articulation and the operation of a particular paradigm on the one hand, and the aims of the project of global constitutionalism as a whole on the other. The next chapter examines precisely how human rights function in global constitutionalism and whether they are able to counter the exclusion/inclusion dynamic.

2

Mechanisms and Modalities of Human Rights in Global Constitutionalism

A Introduction

After having examined the paradigms manifested through such notions as the individual, the state and politics, we can now turn to the fundamental for our inquiry concept of human rights themselves. As will become obvious, the role and functioning of human rights as the foundation of global constitutionalism can only be fully comprehended in light of the previously discussed notions.

In general, the literature on global constitutionalism confidently ascertains the centrality of human rights in the project of global constitutionalism. As mentioned before, for many scholars, human rights represent the ultimate proof that international law is in process of being constitutionalised.[1] However, the nature and type of human rights that through constitutionalisation processes become part of international constitution is considered only in very general terms. Mainly, the discussion focuses on *jus cogens* norms and *erga omnes* obligations without a detailed examination of concrete rights and their content, without examining underlying mechanisms and processes that would allow these rights to fulfil some constitutional functions. Even the nature of these constitutional functions of human rights often remain quite obscure beyond the affirmation of their superior character. In some other instances it would seem that the bulk of international human rights law as a whole is considered to form a part of international constitutionalism.[2] The

[1] The most obvious example is provided by those scholars who base their vision of international constitutionalism on the idea of some shared values. The main representative of this strand is Erika De Wet. See e.g. De Wet, 'Emergence of Value Systems'. Another prominent example is Ernst-Ulrich Petersmann. See e.g. Petersmann, 'Human Rights'.

[2] See e.g. Giegerich, 'The Is and Ought', 37–38, where he takes the UN Charter commitment to human rights as a sign of the constitutionalisation of international law.

diversity of rights guaranteed at the international level triggers a question of the appropriateness and feasibility of such a totalising constitutional value of all human rights. What is specifically constitutional about different rights forming part of the human rights regime apart from their proclaimed orientation towards the protection of human beings? How do different types of human rights function within the constitutionalised international system? Unfortunately, international law scholars – proponents of constitutionalisation – do not discuss these issues.

This chapter presents a more nuanced picture of the functioning of human rights in global constitutionalism. First, a broad overview of various references to human rights in the literature on global constitutionalism is presented. As a next step, the dominant view of human rights in global constitutionalism will be questioned in a twofold manner. Firstly, after an examination of the functioning of constitutional rights within national constitutional orders, a renewed look at human rights as international constitutional rights will allow for questioning the traditional approach that equates human rights with constitutional rights. Secondly, going beyond the traditional approach, more fundamental questions about the purpose and functioning of human rights in global constitutionalism are formulated and examined, combining insights gained in the preceding parts of this chapter.

B State of the Art: Human Rights in International Constitutionalism

The level of generalisation and assumed self-evidence with which human rights are treated as a part of global constitutionalism is well illustrated by the fact that the term 'human rights' is absent from the subject-matter index of one of the most prominent collection of essays on the topic.[3] Although various authors do address human rights as part of their discussion of global constitutionalism,[4] and one essay is even dedicated to human rights and global constitutionalism,[5] the authors neglected to include 'human rights' or even simply 'rights' in the index of their book. It should be noted that such terms as '*jus cogens*', '*erga omnes*' or individual human rights treaties are mentioned in the index, but human rights as a general category is missing. This obviousness with

[3] Dunoff and Trachtman, *Ruling the World.*

[4] See e.g. contributions on human rights by Paulus and Kumm in Dunoff and Trachtman, *Ruling the World.*

[5] Gardbaum, 'Human Rights'.

which human rights are included in the project of constitutionalisation of international law without any further discussion often stands as a barrier to a more detailed and serious examination of the role of human rights and their functioning. The prominent role attributed to the very existence of the notions of *jus cogens* and *erga omnes* represents another impediment.

Firstly, it is remarkable that all authors writing on global constitutionalism agree that respect for some human rights is an indispensable part of any, including global or international, constitutionalisation process.[6] This stands in sharp contrast to ideas expressed by proponents of political constitutionalism – always so far situated within domestic constitutional structures – who in most extreme cases will argue that adequate political mechanisms and arrangements are in themselves a sufficient guarantee of the constitutionalisation of a given society.[7] Less radical proponents of political constitutionalism, while not denying the role rights protection can play within constitutionalism, will regard them as secondary to political mechanisms.[8] They will also be quite precise and selective in determining the range of rights that deserve constitutional status.[9] This confirms the previously made diagnosis of global constitutionalism as a strongly normative phenomenon emerging from within the discipline of international law and influenced by the need for its self-ascertainment. It also confirms the relegation of the political to the subconscious of international law.

A careful investigation of authors' premises reveals that none of the scholars advocating for some type of constitutionalisation of international law will be ready to qualify all human rights as international 'constitutional' rights. More specifically, the fate of socioeconomic rights in the project of constitutionalisation of international law remains a blind spot. So far, no international law scholar working on global constitutionalism has enquired about the possibility of conceptualising socioeconomic rights as a part of a global constitution.[10]

[6] Just to give a few examples: Paulus, 'International Legal System', 71; Kumm, 'Cosmopolitan Turn', 322; O'Donoghue, *Constitutionalism*, 21; Klabbers, Peters and Ulfstein, *Constitutionalization*, 1–3 (the introductory chapter contains no definition of constitutionalism or constitutionalisation but starts with discussion of the use of human rights in various seemingly constitutional contexts).

[7] Most vocally, Bellamy, *Political Constitutinalism.*

[8] See for instance the work of Robert A. Dahl, e.g. Dahl, *Democracy* or more concisely Dahl, 'Political Institutions'.

[9] See e.g. ibid., 188 in particular.

[10] The only exception could be the work of Ernst-Ulrich Petersmann, who in advocating for constitutionalism based on human rights expressly emphasises certain economic rights as

Even within the category of traditional civil and political rights, scholars working on international constitutionalism do not discuss possible differentiation in constitutional role and functions that might be attached to various rights, something that is common in constitutional theory. Taking into account the focus on *erga omnes* and *jus cogens* the range of rights that the majority of defenders of global constitutionalism are ready to qualify as constitutional should be very limited. Equally serious is the omission of the discussion of the nature of rights and their respective constitutional functions, even within the categories of *jus cogens* and *erga omnes*. The content of *jus cogens* and *erga omnes* norms is taken for granted. This in turn raises a series of questions about the nature and unstated presumptions of international constitutionalism as an intellectual movement. In particular, this differentiation of human rights into two groups – those that deserve higher constitutional status, and thus enhanced guarantees, and those that do not deserve this special treatment – introduces an additional layer of hierarchisation into human rights law which at best serves to re-enforce the existing hierarchies and at worst introduces a new one. Since the content and nature of rights and norms that are thus hierarchised is not examined, the process of determining what rights are more important is left to state practice, policy developments and other processes that remain subject to power imbalances and manipulation by more powerful actors. This hierarchisation that adds to the hierarchy introduced by *jus cogens* and *erga omnes* becomes an additional challenge to the theoretically stated indivisibility and equal value of rights.[11] This additional layer of hierarchisation reinforces the cultural bias and paradoxes of human rights that claim to protect the dignity of all human beings equally, but through this hierarchisation and ensuing prioritisation of some human rights, they effectively discard the needs and suffering of large parts of humanity as discussed in the previous chapter.[12]

Hierarchical structure of human rights as part of global constitutionalism signals the presence of the exclusion/inclusion dynamic. Therefore, a more careful and detailed examination of the ways human rights form

being essential to constitutionalisation. See e.g. Ernst-Ulrich Petersmann, 'How to Constitutionalize' and Petersmann, 'Global Compact'.

11 Most prominently stated in Vienna Declaration and Program of Action, 12 July 1993, UN Doc A/CONF 157/23, para 5.

12 See in particular the section on individuals in global constitutionalism and the argument about rights claims being based on the exclusion/inclusion dynamic. This dynamic re-emerges here from a new angle.

part of global constitutionalism, as well as understanding of consequences of various possibilities, is indispensable. The next part of this chapter focuses on examining mechanisms of rights functioning within constitutional systems before turning to the functioning of international human rights.[13] Going beyond a simple affirmation of hierarchical superiority, the below investigation elucidates *how* human rights function.

C Constitutions and the Functioning of Rights: Domestic Experience

1 *Methodological Remarks and the Functioning of Constitutions*

If many discussions around human rights in global constitutionalism operate on the presumption of their similarity to constitutional rights in domestic systems, it is legitimate to enquire about the reason for such a presumption. Is it justified to presume this parallelism? If so, on what grounds? From the perspective of the methodology adopted in this study, the specific perspective from which these questions will be approached is inspired by Deleuze and Guattari's analytical approach to minor literatures. As explained previously, the central question is not what something means, but how it functions. In this light, it is also important to distinguish our interrogation from the traditional functionalist approach in comparative law.[14] Functionalism in comparative law can take a variety of forms. However, the fundamental question a functionalist asks is *what* function fulfils a particular notion or concept.[15] Thus, meaning attributed to functions continues to be the focal point of functionalist analysis. Deleuze and Guattari's approach is different. They investigate *how* the oeuvre in its totality (not its parts) function. Thus, there are two important differences between functionalism in comparative law tradition and

[13] Obviously, today the interrelationship between domestic constitutional rights and international human rights is so close and complex that some authors argue in favour of abandoning this distinction. However, historically protection of constitutional rights within domestic systems emerged first, and the subsequent development of international human rights was greatly influenced by domestic constitutional experience. Therefore, it is not only important to understand this development historically, but also to assess its continuing contemporary relevance.

[14] See e.g. Michaels, 'Functional Method'.

[15] For example, the functional approach to global constitutionalisation adopted by Dunoff and Trachtman also identifies functions based on the 'what' question, namely what functions international constitutional norms fulfil, not the 'how' question. See Dunoff and Trachtman, 'Functional Approach', 10.

Deleuze and Guattari's analysis: first the emphasis shifts from 'what' to 'how'; and second, no division in parts occurs in the sense that although they do investigate different parts of a mechanism, they always simultaneously pay equal attention to connections between parts.

From this perspective, within the below investigation on constitutional rights within domestic systems, the central question will be how rights function as a part of the constitutional order of the society. We will identify the underlying paradigmatic mechanism or mechanisms and then see whether human rights represent a similar mechanism at the international level. The analysis will proceed by establishing parallels to domestic constitutionalism, an approach that was criticised from the outset of this study. However, as will become clear towards the end of this chapter, this approach is used differently here: not to orient international constitutionalism towards mimicking of domestic experiences but to place the discourse on global constitutionalism in a new light. It is equally important to highlight that this section is not concerned with divers domestic constitutional rights experiences in a technical legal sense. In order to get insights into the fundamental paradigmatic mechanisms of rights protection within states, a sociological approach that draws on experiences from different states but paints a general picture is more useful. Within sociology, there exists a certain ambiguity with regard to fundamental rights. Writing as recently as 2013, Gert Verschraegen starts his analysis of a possible sociological approach to fundamental rights with the statement that 'most pundits agree that by and large, sociologists have not developed a general theory of fundamental rights.'[16] Nevertheless, works of several contemporary sociologists provide better insights into the paradigmatic mechanisms of fundamental rights than analyses by political scientists or lawyers.[17]

The existing sociological theories of fundamental rights all draw in one way or another on the idea of social differentiation within Luhmann's systems theory.[18] This idea postulates that as the environment of a particular system becomes more complex, the system tends to undergo

[16] Verschraegen, 'Differentiation and Inclusion', 61.

[17] For a useful explanation of insufficiencies of these approaches that the present author shares see e.g. Thornhill, 'Rights and Constituent Power', 371–372; Madsen and Verschraegen 'Making Human Rights Intelligible', 5–11.

[18] The two main sociologists who developed this theory are Talcott Parsons and Niklas Luhmann. However, it goes back to some ideas developed in relation to functional differentiation by Emile Durkheim. The three main contemporary authors extending this theory more specifically to the issue of human rights and constitutionalism are Gunter Teubner, Chris Thornhill and Gert Verschraegen.

a process of differentiation through the creation of subsystems.[19] Each subsystem is responsible for a particular function. Within society, one particular subsystem is the political system. This system fulfils the function of problem solving in society through binding decisions.[20] Luhmann emphasises that the state as the political system is one of many function-specific subsystems that presupposes the existence of other subsystems side by side with itself.[21] As far as the legal system is concerned, one particular fundamental point relates to norm production. On this sociological view norm production is not regarded as a result of rational interpersonal deliberations but as emerging from within the functional needs of a system.[22]

It should also be emphasised that while Luhmann's theory broadly forms a basis for different views that will be considered here, each author has his or her own understanding of this theory and reinterprets and modifies it, at times to a considerable degree. Therefore, particular care is required when drawing on writings of different authors. In what follows, I focus on works of Luhmann and Thornhill.[23] The choice of Luhmann's work is obvious due to him being the founding father of this functional differentiation theory, which he discussed in much detail in relation to the state. However, it was important to complement it with the works of Thornhill, who, based on Luhmann's heritage, provided a very detailed theorisation focusing specifically on constitutions and rights both in domestic legal systems and at the global level.

One fundamental difference between the approaches of Luhmann and Thornhill to be highlighted from the outset relates to their view of the relationship between the political and the legal systems. For Luhmann, in the modern differentiated society the legal and the political system are two separate systems. These two systems have their internal logic and a specific function. The fundamental binary code with which the legal system operates is that of legal and illegal,[24] whereas the political system's

[19] For a general but brief overview of the idea of social differentiation see Luhmann, 'Differentiation in Society'.

[20] Luhmann, *Grundrechte*, 14. [21] Ibid., 15.

[22] The importance of this aspect is emphasised in Thornhill, 'Rights and Constituent Power', 359; Verschraegen, 'Differentiation and Inclusion', 69.

[23] It should be signalled already here that the works of Teubner are also considered when discussing the functioning of international human rights. However, since Teubner did not expressly develop his theory for the nation-state setting, his works are not discussed in this part dealing with fundamental rights in domestic settings.

[24] Luhmann, *Law*, 174.

code is based on the distinction powerful/powerless (*Macht/Ohnmacht*).[25] These systems, however, do not exist in complete isolation from each other. Luhmann describes the relationship between these two systems through the concept of structural coupling. Technically speaking, structural coupling is the way a particular system regulates its relationship to its environment.[26] However, since the political system is part of the environment of the legal system and vice versa,[27] we can affirm that the concept of structural coupling describes the relationship between the two systems. The main function of a structural coupling is to reduce and at the same time facilitate the influences of the environment on the system.[28] The particular form of the structural coupling that is formed between law and politics is the 'state' or, more precisely, the state that is given a constitution.[29] Thus, the constitutional state is what entertains the relationship between the legal and the political, whereas constitution that constitutes and defines the state has different meanings within each system: 'For the legal system it is a supreme statute, a basic law. For the political system it is an instrument of politics, in the double sense of both instrumental politics (which changes states of affairs) and symbolic politics (which does not).'[30] As far as the legal system is concerned, an important function of the constitution is to normalise and limit the political influence on law.[31]

Thornhill, in contrast, views political and legal systems as homogenous.[32] Therefore, he might view differently the particular mechanism that the constitution puts in motion. In particular, in his analysis of the role of constitutions from the perspective of sociological theory, he places a very strong emphasis on constitutions as formative of the political system.[33] In defining the political function he also places more emphasis

[25] Luhmann, 'Verfassungen', 193; in another context he uses the terms '*Machtueberlegenheit/Machtunterlegenheit*' (Luhmann, *Politik*, 88). On the role of power as a medium of the political system, see Luhmann, *Politik*, 18–68; on the binary coding of the political system, see ibid., 88–102; on legal/illegal, Luhmann, *Law*, 93, 173–210.

[26] Luhmann, *Law*, 381. [27] Ibid., 381–384.

[28] Ibid., 382. Interestingly, Luhmann describes the development of law itself as 'a function of the social system in relation to a problem, which arises within the structural coupling of this system with its environment' (ibid., 384) that then becomes itself a system. The particular problem within a social system that law addresses is 'the stabilization of normative expectations by regulating how they are generalized in relation to their temporal, factual, and social dimensions'. Ibid., 148. For more details on this, see ibid., Chapter 3.

[29] Ibid., 404. [30] Ibid., 410. [31] Luhmann, 'Verfassungen' 190.

[32] Thornhill, 'Rights and Constituent Power' 358.

[33] Thornhill, *Transnational Constitutions*, 29.

on the political system's capacity to generate authority and produce decisions, than on its dealing with power.[34] In Thornhill's view the political system is underpinned by an inclusionary structure that acts as a reservoir of normative legitimacy for the political system.[35] Constitution is the legally articulated form of society's inclusionary structure (which is part of the political system).[36] Constitutions in Thornhill's view are not tied to states or nations but to the political system:[37] 'constitutional law as a set of norms that are adaptively produced, under particular circumstances, by society's need to preserve a distinctive political domain'.[38] As a consequence, this fundamental role of constitutions as mechanisms of coupling between the legal and the political systems of the society disappears from Thornhill's view. Although the idea that constitutions act as mechanisms that allow the political system to maintain its identity or to be differentiated form other systems is shared by both, Luhmann's view is more complex in that for him a constitution differentiates not only the political system from the rest of the social subsystems but the legal system from the political system – and at the same time, both of them from other systems. Let's now consider in more detail the role of the constitution and then more specifically the role and mechanism of fundamental rights protection.

The social differentiation theory views the state and its institutions, including constitutional protection of rights in a way that departs from many traditional accounts, including those dominant among international lawyers. One of the central arguments defended by sociologists working within the tradition of social-functional differentiation relates to the state and its power. Whereas the dominant view represents the state as ascribing to itself and concentrating in its hands more and more power, including through law, the theory of social differentiation emphasises that modern states or modern political systems emerge through the process of functional differentiation that entails abandoning some power to other subsystems within a given society. If states as political systems would monopolise all the power, they would simply discredit themselves and collapse as a result of being unable to manage all the complexity of social interactions:

> The abstraction and generalisation of power around emergent states actually formed part of a process in which states developed as institutions that *limited* society's political accountability to determinate and discrete societal functions, and that actively *curtailed* the use of political power in spheres of society that had no immediate requirement for it.[39]

[34] Ibid., 2. [35] Ibid., 5. [36] Ibid., 7. [37] Ibid., 29. [38] Ibid., 30.
[39] Thornhill, 'State Building', 31, emphasis in the original.

In this process of defining and delimiting political power, law, and constitutional law more specifically, played and continues to play a central role: '[T]he modern political system has an internally formative relation to legal norms, and it evolves and consolidates itself as a modern political system because of this inner correlation with the body of positive law.'[40]

Within the context of this process, constitutional norms formation could be said to have played a twofold role: that of political abstraction[41] and societal depoliticisation.[42] In their function of political abstraction, constitutional norms helped states to 'outline and stabilise the parameters of the political function'.[43] As far as societal depoliticisation is concerned, the central element consists in the ability of constitutional orders 'politically to include and exclude their citizens in the same act, to legitimise themselves as political through this act and to effectively (or paradoxically) limit their politicality by claiming inclusivity as the ground for their legitimacy'.[44] Through this process where constitutions play a central role, states establish themselves as political and legitimate.

2 *Specifics of Fundamental Rights Functioning*

Within constitutions, fundamental rights protection is one of the cornerstone foundations. Therefore, what was said above about the functioning of constitutions, to some degree, equally applies to constitutional rights. However, since rights represent only a portion of constitutions, the question of their specific functioning as distinct from constitutions as a whole can legitimately be raised. The most systematic and detailed sociological attempt so far remains Luhmann's.[45] His theory created the basis for some contemporary elaborations that, while building on Luhmann's foundations, often go further and diverge from his original ideas.[46] The foundational theses of Luhmann's approach that are of particular relevance for the present work can be summarised as follows. Firstly, constitutional rights emerge as a response to the process of functional differentiation in complex societies.[47] Secondly, against the widely held

[40] Ibid., 39. [41] Ibid., 42–46.

[42] Ibid., 46–51, See also generally Chris Thornhill, *Constitutions*, 372–376; Luhmann, 'Verfassungen'.

[43] Thornhill, 'State Building', 43. [44] Ibid., 48.

[45] The main reference here is Luhmann, *Grundrechte*. His other works on law and, more specifically, constitutions also address this topic.

[46] Most prominently, see the works of Thornhill, but also Verschraegen.

[47] See Luhmann, *Grundrechte* generally and Chapter 2 more specifically.

view of human rights as protections against state power, 'fundamental rights are not only directed against state action, but protect individual and social autonomy against the expansive dynamics of other social systems as well'.[48] Finally, rights operate as a mechanism of individuals' inclusion in various social systems.[49]

Thus, contrary to the widespread perception among international lawyers, fundamental rights are first of all not a legal phenomenon – not even in the sense of natural law – but a factual need, a pre-legal social expectation that only later is stabilised and articulated in law.[50] Fundamental rights primarily operate not as protectors of the individual but as mechanisms that simultaneously constitute individuals as, for example, worthy of dignity, in need of work or education, and constitute particular social subsystems as differentiated, and thus unsubsumable under politics or other social subsystems. However, the political system of society represents a particular danger, according to Luhmann, because the differentiated political order tends to instability and can lead to an unexpected eruption of the political beyond its setting that can lead to de-differentiation.[51] The institution of constitutional rights protection represents the primary and most efficient mechanism to maintain social differentiation.[52]

A further important element in understanding fundamental rights as a mechanism preventing social de-differentiation is the emphasis Luhmann places on communication in the context of social differentiation.[53] According to Luhmann, human rights differentiate types of communication, not groups of persons. In modern differentiated society, individuals do not belong to one single social subsystem exclusively.[54] They can participate equally in a number of social subsystems, or can change from one subsystem to another.[55] However, communication within each subsystem is different. Therefore, to maintain the mobility of persons across different social subsystems, there is a need for mechanisms that allow for the generalisation of communication.[56] Fundamental

48 Verschraegen, 'Differentiation and Inclusion', 68.

49 Luhmann, 'Subjektive Rechte', 84–85. 50 Luhmann, *Grundrechte*, 12–13.

51 Ibid., 23–24.

52 Ibid., 24. He also mentions separation of powers as one of the best-known mechanisms, and separation of politics and administration as one of the most efficient. He highlights however the pre-eminence of fundamental rights: 'Allen voran ist jedoch die Institution des Grundrechte zu nennen, die von der neueren deutschen Verfassungslehre mit Recht in den Mittelpunkt ihrer Staatskonzeption gestellt wird.'

53 See in particular ibid., 34–37. 54 Luhmann, 'Individuum', 158. 55 Ibid.

56 Luhmann, *Grundrechte*, 37. He identifies at least the four following areas where differentiation through these generalising mechanisms should be guaranteed: self-

rights prevent corruption of these mechanisms through the political system.[57] Thus, fundamentally for Luhmann, the individual in the modern differentiated society is defined through exclusion: exclusion from the society as such that is needed in order to open up a possibility of inclusion into different social subsystems.[58] Therefore, for Luhmann, the individual can best be defined as a system for which the society is its environment.[59] In this regard Luhmann stands apart from much of the legal scholarship but also from many sociological theories. Mostly, the individual and society is theorised through the idea of inclusion, however imperfect.[60] In other instances, scholars overemphasise the element of inclusion without abandoning the exclusionary role of rights.[61] In yet other instances inclusion is too encompassing. For example, many scholars, including sociologists, define society through the inclusion of individuals as its members, for instance based on citizenship, a society that in turn is viewed as a type of community with a common cultural framework.[62] In contrast, for Luhmann, fundamental rights work as mechanisms of exclusion first, and as delineating inclusion only secondarily. Moreover, they delineate inclusion in particular social subsystems only, not the society as a whole. Therefore, he interprets the concept of citizenship as inclusion in the political system only.[63] Thus, fundamental rights signal only the *possibility* for individuals to participate in various social subsystems.

In this vision fundamental rights emerge as a mechanism with its proper functioning within a machine of interconnected mechanisms. It becomes clear that fundamental rights function in a way that contributes to the construction and maintenance of the state, of the political system, but also construct and maintain a particular vision of life and meaning of life for human beings. Fundamental rights represent a mechanism embedded in a complex structure that is constantly moving and affecting all other components of this structure. Thus, if constitutions are best

representation of a person; formation of reliable expectations of behaviour; satisfaction of economic needs, and the possibility of reaching binding decisions in common.

57 Ibid.

58 This idea is developed and most clearly articulated with all its consequences in Luhmann, 'Individuum'. For instance, he states, 'Das Individuum kann nicht meh durch Inklusion, sondern nur noch durch Exklusion definiert werden.' (Ibid., 158).

59 Ibid.

60 Durkheim, *Leçons de sociologie*; Parsons, 'Full Citizenship'; Smend 'Verfassung', 265.

61 Thornhill, *Transnational Constitutions*, 4–5, 19; 59–60 (switches to the language of selection instead of exclusion).

62 See for example Parsons, *Societies* in general.

63 Luhmann, *Law*, 363.

understood in the relationship between the political and the legal system in the image of a structural coupling that allows each of the two systems to communicate with its environment while maintaining its identity as a separate system, then fundamental rights fulfil a broader function that directly implicates the individual. Fundamental rights constitute individuals as social systems (thus autonomous, independent and able to be self-sufficient), while at the same time allowing this individual to move between different social subsystems (not only between the legal and the political, but also the economic, the cultural and so on). In the same way that an individual is structured by fundamental rights as autonomous, simultaneously fundamental rights support the maintenance of autonomy in all social subsystems. Although, as Luhmann noted, the expansionist tendencies of the political system are particularly dangerous, therefore we can say that fundamental rights focus on preventing the de-differentiation of the political system more than of any other social system.

The above analysis was introduced with the main purpose of demonstrating the falsity of the vision of fundamental rights as barriers protecting individuals against the state or against abuse of power by state actors. While fundamental rights are occasionally used to protect individuals against state intrusion, this is just a peripheral, marginal or even accidental role they happen to play, not their main reason for existence.

In order to reinforce this thesis, an additional example from the US constitutional experience is discussed below. The particular debate that is of interest relates to the discussion about the need to include a bill of rights into a federal constitution that took place between 1787, when the text of a new constitution was proposed without a bill of rights, and the adoption of the Bill of Rights in 1791. The situation involved a net of historical circumstances that cannot be detailed here.[64] However, several arguments raised during the debates over the introduction of the Bill of Rights point out that the Bill of Rights is not the primary mechanism protecting citizens from abuses of power by the government. They also confirm that the need to protect citizens against abuses of power by the government was not the main reason for the introduction of the Bill of Rights.

It is remarkable that the person who is often credited with being 'the Father of the Bill of Rights', James Madison, for a long period of time[65]

[64] For an overview see e.g. Les Benedict, *The Blessings of Liberty*, 63–88; Nardo, *Creation*, 75–89; and more focused Rutland, *Birth of the Bill.*

[65] It could be said that he was opposed to the idea of a bill of rights at least until 1789, but then his opinion evolved slowly. On this see Morgan, *Madison*, 131. This book generally provides a good overview of Madison's opinions presented here, in particular Chapter 6.

defended the view that a bill of rights is not needed in order to protect people from the abuse of power by the government. He held the view that a well-structured government with checks and balances, separation of powers and precisely prescribed powers is a better guarantee against abuse of power than any bill of rights.[66] He equally defended the view that the ease with which the government can abuse its power depends on the nature of majorities that are formed. In order to prevent the abuse of power, it was essential to prevent divisions between the majority and the minority on a single issue, particularly a moral one. This is best achieved not through a bill of rights but through a particular structure of society that needed to promote diversity and representation of a variety of interests and parties.[67] Madison was pushed to change his position on the issue of the Bill of Rights and even to become the drafter of and an advocate for the Bill of Rights under pressure of external factors, including public opinion and the danger that, without the Bill of Rights, the constitution would not get sufficient support.[68]

Equally significant is the fact that the Bill of Rights played almost no role in securing rights for more than a century of US constitutional history.[69] This indicates that, as Madison initially argued, other mechanisms related to the structure and powers of government and legislature are well suited to protect individuals against abuses of power by the state and the fact that inclusion of fundamental right into constitutions is a pragmatic choice. If we remember the strong influence exercised by the US on the idea of international human rights,[70] we need to seriously consider how far the thesis of the power-limiting function of human

[66] This is particularly clear from his co-authorship of the Federalist Papers. One of them, Federalist No. 84, is particularly outspoken on the topic. Although the author of this paper is Hamilton and not Madison himself, the fact that the Federalist Papers were first published under a pseudonym ('Publius'), thus representing them as written by one single person, indicates Madison's acceptance and agreement with these views. For an interesting discussion of this argument see Berns, 'Constitution', 50–73.

[67] For this argument, see in particular Federalist No. 10, which was authored by Madison.

[68] For a short overview: Rutland, 'How the Constitution Protects'. For a more detailed account: Labunski, *Madison*, Chapter 7 in particular; see also Morgan, *Madison*, Chapter 6.

[69] See e.g. Berns, 'Constitution', 52. If we look at specific rights that were held to be very important during the discussion of the need for a bill of rights, such as religious liberty, the picture is even more surprising: 'The religious liberty enjoyed by Americans owed nothing to judicial enforcement of the First Amendment . . . not once during those first 136 years did the Supreme Court invalidate an act of Congress on First Amendment grounds. (It did not do so until . . . 1971 in a religion case.)' Ibid.

[70] As Louis Henkin puts it, 'The United States has also been the principal exponent of making the idea of rights universal as well as international.' Henkin, 'Constitutionalism', 384.

rights holds. The next section will examine whether human rights function similarly to the fundamental rights in national legal orders and, if no, how do they function.

D Beyond the Domestic Constitutional Experience

1 Approaching the Functioning of Human Rights from a Sociological Perspective

The question of how human rights function cannot be answered with the same level of clarity and easiness that was present in the answer to the similar question posed in relation to fundamental rights in domestic constitutional systems in the previous section. The examination of mechanisms underlying the functioning of human rights is complicated by various factors that include, without being limited to, the higher level of complexity of systems present at the international or global level, pervasiveness and invisibility of state thinking as well as less elaborate and less extensive literature that results from the previous two factors. In relation to this latter factor, it suffices to point out at this stage that well into the twentieth century, sociological theories despite their willingness to extend the applicability of rights to the whole of humanity were not able to show 'what could serve as the necessary equivalent to the national societal community in the international system'.[71] From the outset we see how the question of human rights is linked to both the political and the state paradigm, as discussed in the previous chapter. The link between the paradigm of individual and human rights is more obvious due to the rhetoric of protection inherent in human rights, but it is more difficult to discern beyond this rhetoric.

Luhmann's own analysis of the global from the perspective of his social systems theory is significantly less detailed and thorough as compared to the application of his theory to states as organising units of society.[72] This does not mean, however, as some authors argue, that

[71] Verschraegen, 'Differentiation and Inclusion', 75 and discussion on this page; see also more broadly on difficulties of the contemporary sociological theories with addressing the extension of constitutional thinking to the global realm, a diagnosis that this author shares, in Thornhill, 'Luhmann'.

[72] For example, in Luhmann's book *Law as a Social System*, the discussion of law in relation to the global realm occupies only 11 out of 490 pages. Similarly, his other works do not leave the idea of the global society (*Weltgesellschaft*) and its plurality out of consideration. They simply devote less space and attention to these topics but treat them as part and parcel of his elaborations of different aspects of the systems theory.

Luhmann's system-theoretical methodology cannot accurately interpret the global society.[73] It's simply that there is a need for more interpretative effort because some aspects of Luhmann's theory in relation to the global realm are not articulated as clearly and with as much detail as some other aspects. Therefore, in order to supply a consistent basis for comparison with the functioning of rights in domestic systems, this chapter again takes Luhmann's theory as he himself articulated it in relation to the global realm as its point of departure. However, other visions, in particular interpretations and extensions of his theory by Thornhill and Teubner, are also introduced. The conclusion will be drawn against the backdrop of these various visions of the mechanism of human rights as it functions at the global level.

2 *How Human Rights Function within the Global Context: Three Possible Answers*

a) Luhmann and Two Ways

From the outset, it is important to emphasise that for Luhmann there is no doubt that whatever concept of society one adopts, there is today only one society: the global society.[74] He holds that it is unsuitable to talk about national 'systems', as it is not possible to delineate these national systems as systems, and territorial borders 'are singularly unsuited to deal with this issue'.[75] Equally problematic for him is the use of the term 'international system'[76] or 'global system'.[77] Global society is the result of a 'worldwide interweaving of all functioning systems'.[78]

An interesting insight into the nature of global society relates to Luhmann's diagnosis of global society as being more receptive to cognitive expectations and mechanisms as opposed to normative.[79] This is insofar peculiar, as social systems usually have preference for the normative pattern of forming expectations because they are easier to institutionalise.[80] The difference between the cognitive and the normative patterns can be summarised as follows: cognitive expectations have as their object

[73] Fischer-Lescano, 'Die Emergenz', 720.

[74] Luhmann, *Law*, 479. Luhmann uses the term '*Weltgesellschaft*' (see for example Luhmann, *Recht*, 671), which is better translated as 'world society'. However, keeping in line with the dominant linguistic usage, the term 'global society' is used here.

[75] Luhmann, *Law*, 480.

[76] Ibid, See also Luhmann, *Politik*, 222; Luhmann, 'Weltgesellschaft', 57.

[77] Luhmann, *Politik*, 220. [78] Luhmann, *Law*, 480.

[79] Luhmann, 'Weltgesellschaft', 55. [80] Ibid., 56–57.

themselves and can learn and change themselves, while normative expectation are directed at something external and instead of learning and changing themselves, they change the object at which they are directed.[81] This difference in the way global society works raises the question of the continuing relevance or at least primacy of law and politics at the global level. Luhmann in this connection raises the question of the need for other mechanisms that allow the institutionalisation of cognitive learning at the global level.[82] Luhmann also questions the transferability of the phenomenon of regional integration at the global level because it represents a peculiar combination of law and politics whereby the political stabilises in the face of 'dangers' through the formation of groups and opposing interests, therefore it can never encompass the entire globe.[83] This diagnosis of the political system also confirms that the dominant paradigm of the political is still Schmittean. Luhmann is clearly assertive about the existence of the political and the legal system of the global society.[84] These systems, in contrast to other functional systems, remain dependant on the state form or, as Luhmann says, 'regionally differentiable in the form of States'.[85] Despite the centrality of the state form, he equally emphasises that typical for the global society are heterarchical, network-type connections that he affirms will only increase.[86]

Luhmann acknowledges the existence of the global political system, despite its continuing reliance on the state form. Thus, for instance he affirms that 'the global political system . . . makes states enter into indissoluble dependencies on each other and do this in view of the ecological consequences of modern warfare with the compelling logic of prevention and intervention.'[87] The political system emerged when it was differentiated as a subsystem of the global society. It then secondarily and internally differentiated itself into states.[88] The need for this secondary differentiation was brought about for several reasons, among them the need to prevent the politicisation of other functional systems, but at the same time it works as a mechanism promoting globalisation of other functional systems.[89] Also, it is meaningful to differentiate the political system by regions (states) because in this way it can relate better to the local condition.[90]

[81] Ibid., 55. [82] Ibid., 59–60. [83] Ibid., 57.
[84] See in particular Luhmann, *Law* and Luhmann, *Politik* in general.
[85] 'Regional differenzierbar in der Form von Staaten . . . ' Luhmann, *Gesellschaft*, 166.
[86] Luhmann, *Politik*, 221. [87] Luhmann, *Law*, 480. [88] Luhmann, *Politik*, 222.
[89] Ibid., 223–224. [90] Luhmann, *Law*, 484.

Luhmann explicitly affirms the existence of the legal order of the global society despite the absence of central legislation and decision-making.[91] Attention paid to human rights violations is for him one of the most important indicators of the global legal system.[92] However, he also states that

> The legal system remains state law or law based on treaties between states. Accordingly, states are expected to be responsible for their compliance with human rights on their territories and the rights themselves appear as a requirement of state legislation and state enforcement.[93]

Thus, Luhmann highlights both convergences that indicate the existence of the global legal system, and the differences that persist. He relativises the differences,[94] but nevertheless he affirms that 'The legal system of global society is in many respects a special case.'[95] Finally, Luhmann sees the global legal system as developing in close relationship with the global political system. This is exactly the same pattern that we observed in his description of the legal and the political systems at the domestic level. With regard to the global legal system and its relationship to the global political system, he highlights that, despite regional and cultural differences, no one contests the need for 'legal protection against the arbitrariness of states'.[96] This for him exemplifies a discrepancy between the legal and the political that first appeared in Europe but now unfolds globally in a variety of forms due to the spread of the state form across the globe.[97]

As we have seen, when discerning the legal system of the global society, Luhmann pays particular attention to human rights. However, his view on the role of human rights in this regard departs from the traditional widespread view of human rights as protections of individuals against abuses of power or guarantees of individual freedom. He affirms,

> To define the function of law as an instrument securing freedom has, as do all definitions of function, hardly any interpretative value. This applies also to human rights . . . which are hardly at the disposition of individuals. Accordingly, they cannot be understood as subjective rights. Human rights are definitely a result of modern individualism, but disobedience of the law is an equally important result as well.[98]

Here Luhmann point out one potentially very important difference between fundamental rights in domestic constitutional systems and human rights. As we have seen in the previous section, fundamental

[91] Ibid., 481. [92] Ibid., 482. [93] Ibid., 483. [94] Ibid., 481. [95] Ibid. [96] Ibid., 483.
[97] Ibid., 484. [98] Ibid., 479.

rights constitute individuals as subjects, thus Luhmann also describes them as subjective rights.[99] However, here Luhmann highlights the impossibility of conceiving human rights as subjective rights.[100]

When describing how human rights are relevant at the global level, Luhmann emphasises that human rights do not benefit from textual clarity or precision but from the evidence of human rights violations. In other words, the reference to and invocation of human rights appears when the global society witnesses horrific events in which the unacceptability of their occurrence is beyond question. But in this situation, to a large degree it becomes irrelevant what rights, principles or texts to invoke. Therefore, he affirms the continuing symbolic role of human rights similar to the role of fundamental rights in domestic constitutional systems.[101] However, according to Luhmann, even this symbolic role of human rights is ruined by its inflation.[102] One of the examples he uses relates to the emergence of welfare states and socioeconomic rights that are conceived as a provision of care and supply of goods that extend responsibility from those who 'break the law *stricto sensu*' to those 'who can provide help'.[103] Taking into account difficulties with implementing and ensuring compliance with this type of rights, it becomes even more normal that human rights will not be taken seriously. This in turn shifts attention from human rights violations as such to the *most severe* human rights violations. Therefore, the guarantee of a functioning rule of law and respect for human rights become almost synonymous,[104] thus depriving human rights even of this symbolic role.

According to Luhmann, what unfolds in human rights is a paradox of the relationship between the law and the individual.[105] From the perspective of human rights today, 'it is also a paradox to say that rights are only implemented by their violation and the corresponding outrage.'[106] In face of this paradox he formulates two suggestions, both of which are in a conditional form. Since there is no certainty about how the system will develop itself in response to particular difficulties, he can only formulate some thoughts and suggestions, not certainties about the

[99] Luhmann, *Grundrechte*, 30; on the idea of subjective rights see Luhmann, 'Subjektive Rechte'.

[100] At another place he also highlights again the insufficiency of viewing human rights as subjective rights because they cannot be invoked freely: Luhmann, *Law*, 486.

[101] Ibid., 484. [102] Ibid., 485. [103] Ibid., 484–485. [104] Ibid., 485–486.

[105] For more on the paradox inherent in human rights see Luhmann, 'Paradox der Menschenrechte'.

[106] Luhmann, *Law*, 487.

future. However, taking into account Luhmann's familiarity with the functioning of highly differentiated social systems, it is very important to take into account and reflect upon his suggestions. These two suggestions are contrasting because if the first one points towards a possibility of the maintenance of a global normative system, the second idea proposes that in the long run, the society's need to rely on legal coding will disappear.

(1) Maintaining a Global Normative System In relation to the fact that human rights become relevant today through their violation, Luhmann suggests that this is perhaps what is appropriate in our turbulent times. However, simultaneously this could mark, according to Luhmann, an end of the discussion of the relevance of the specific European tradition in the sense that 'a global society, which is scandalised sufficiently by gross failures, could be expected to establish a structure of legal norms, independent of regional traditions and the political interests of regional states.'[107] Thus, the first possibility is actually very much in line with the aspirations of many proponents of global constitutionalism since it points out into a direction of a common global normative structure independent of regional variations. This possibility was developed and discussed by Fischer-Lescano, who places the process of scandalisation in face of human rights violations at the centre of his elaboration of a global constitution.[108]

Luhmann, however views this possibility with ambiguity. He points out that despite all developments linked to globalisation, the regional differences do not disappear due to the secondary differentiation of the political system in 'states'.[109] The crucial consequence of this continuing secondary differentiation of the political system 'is that the structural coupling of the political system and the legal system through constitutions does not have an equivalent at the level of global society'.[110] However, even this absence of the structural coupling between law and politics at the global level does not provide sufficient explanation for divergent developments that go so far as to lead us to question the very functionality of law at the global level.

Thus, in this response to his own suggestion that the global normative system freed from regional variations is possible, Luhmann affirms three things: (1) the absence of a constitution in a functional sense at the global

[107] Ibid., 487. [108] Fischer-Lescano, *Globalverfassung*. [109] Luhmann, *Law*, 487.
[110] Ibid., 487–488.

level, and (2) without denying the possibility of the maintenance and further development of a global structure of legal norms he highlights a fundamental difficulty this process is inevitably facing; furthermore, and this is crucial for the arguments advanced in this study, (3) the absence of the structural coupling between politics and law at the global level is due to the differentiation of the political system in states. Thus, Luhmann's identification of the impediments to the constitutionalisation of the global realm is very much in line with the diagnosis and proposals made in the previous chapter in relation to paradigms of global constitutionalism. It particularly highlights the need to overcome the state form.

(2) Disappearance of the Need for Law In trying to consider in more detail the reasons for this fundamental difficulty faced by the global normative system on the way towards its further convergence beyond outrage in face of most serious human rights violations, Luhmann comes up with his second suggestion. Luhmann starts by stating that this difficulty might be related to the fact that large parts of populations are not included in the communication of functioning systems or, in other words, due to a stark difference between exclusion and inclusion.[111] Exclusion and inclusion are produced by functional differentiation, but in the case at hand, the consequences of exclusion or inclusion are so extreme that exclusion/inclusion code overwrites all other codes, including the legal/illegal code of law.[112] Also, the exclusion means better integration and thus less freedom, while inclusion is associated with less integration and thus more freedom.[113] If the inclusion of some depends on the exclusion of others, which according to Luhmann is inevitable,[114] this difference undermines the normal functioning of functional systems[115] and in particular law. This is what might be happening at the global level with regional variations in wealth, access to resources, etc. It's not a matter of development and just waiting and doing something, but perhaps attaining the level of welfare comparable to most wealthy Western states might not be possible at the global level.

> Therefore it may well be that the current prominence of the legal system and the dependence of society itself and of most of its functional systems

[111] Ibid., 488. [112] Ibid., 489. [113] Ibid., 489.
[114] See in particular discussion in Luhmann, 'Inklusion und Exklusion'.
[115] Luhmann, *Law*, 490.

> on a functioning legal coding are nothing but a European anomaly, which might well level off with the evolution of global society.[116]

Thus, Luhmann's second suggestion is very far reaching and points to the disappearance of the legal. Significantly, the exclusion/inclusion dynamic, which was highlighted in the previous chapter's analysis of existing paradigms of the individual and the state within global constitutionalism, emerges in Luhmann's analysis. As stated this contradiction ultimately impedes the project of global constitutionalism. Here Luhmann gets very close to some of the ideas discussed by Agamben, who suggests that the new community, the coming community and the coming politics have to take non-statal and non-legal form.[117] This disappearance of the legal is also implied in Luhmann's own discussion of the global society as being more sensitive to the cognitive form of expectations' formation than to the normative one.[118]

(3) Summary and Transition The above analysis of the functioning of human rights at the global level through the prism of Luhmann's systems theory brings to light the following points: First, unlike fundamental rights within domestic constitutions, human rights cannot be conceived as subjective rights. From this we can infer that human rights do function differently as compared to fundamental rights, at least in relation to the individual. Second, although Luhmann identifies two possible developments within the global social system as far its legal subsystem is concerned, he clearly affirms that in its present state the global society lacks the structural coupling between law and politics, which is fundamental for the existence of a constitution. If there is no constitution in the form of the structural coupling at the global level, there can be no fundamental rights at the global level. Therefore, the functioning of human rights is different from the functioning of fundamental rights in domestic systems. Finally, Luhmann suggests that the future of global society overcoming the exclusion/inclusion dynamic brought about by differentiation in states could lie in ordering without law and human rights.

However, as we have seen, Luhmann's own theory does not articulate very clearly the place of human rights from the perspective of functional differentiation. In this context we need to examine two influential sociological theories constructed as an extension of Luhmann's work that deal

[116] Ibid. [117] See Chapter 1, section 'Politics of Global Constitutionalism'.
[118] See above section 'Luhmann and Two Ways'.

with constitutions at the global level and human rights more specifically before being able to make any conclusions as to the functioning of human rights within global constitutionalism. These theories have been developed by Chris Thornhill and Gunter Teubner.

b) Thornhill and the Fusion of Law and Politics

Thornhill's discussion of the constitution of the global society starts from a premise identical to that of Luhmann, namely that 'modern society is in the process of evolving a global political system'.[119] He affirms that since constitutions as the society's inclusionary structure are not tied to the state form but to a political system,[120] as the political system evolves, constitutions evolve too. According to Thornhill, the constitution of the global society is more adequately described as a transnational one because it is located 'partly within and partly outside national societies'.[121] In this he proposes a new perspective that departs from both the traditional international law scholarship on global constitutionalism and the postnational pluralist scholarship. In this regard he also transcends the traditional distinction between domestic and international processes without eliminating it.[122] For instance, in relation to human rights he affirms that they

> are generated by inner-societal pressures and claims for inclusion, and, once internalised in domestic legal systems, they greatly enhance the inclusionary structure of domestic societies, allowing national political institutions to function more autonomously and more effectively.[123]

Thus, human rights are also more adequately described today as transnational rights.[124] He also strongly emphasises the inclusionary

[119] Thornhill, *Transnational Constitutions*, 1. [120] See text at note 39.
[121] Thornhill, *Transnational Constitutions*, 9.
[122] See e.g. Ibid., 22–30 for a summary of his argument on this point. [123] Ibid., 19.
[124] To be more precise, Thornhill himself distinguishes international human rights from transnational rights. However, this distinction is not entirely clear. In the subject index, the term 'transnational rights' refers to five occurrences on six pages, all of them being reduced to a simple description of how transnational rights support different processes within the global society without clarifying precisely how these transnational rights are distinct form international human rights. The only exception is on page 418 where transnational rights are described as being constructed 'through multiple inter-judicial interactions'. It seems therefore that depending on one's particular vision of what is included into human rights law and how human rights law is constructed, what Thornhill means by transnational rights can still fall under the rubric of international human rights. I think here Thornhill wanted to emphasise a particular functionality emerging within human rights regime and therefore chose this distinct terminology. For the purposes of this study the term 'international human rights' or simply 'human rights'

function of human rights. The exclusionary function of human rights that mirrors the exclusionary function of fundamental rights is mentioned a few times,[125] as is the fact that the rise of global constitutional norms enhances the capacity of states to deal with power.[126] However, the inclusionary function emerges as dominant in his discussions. When following the historical development of international law and human rights, Thornhill formulates a distinct vision of the role of human rights. Central to his argument is the displacement of the conceptual basis of legitimacy from the idea of constituent power to human rights.[127] This fact signalled a revision of the inclusionary structure of society. It also signified that the inclusionary mechanism of the society is formed not by traditional national constitutions based on the link between constituent power and right but by international human rights as developed and articulated by international courts, tribunals and quasi-judiciary bodies.[128]

These arguments seem quite plausible and explain many processes taking place at the global level better than pre-existing theories, including several sociological versions. However, Thornhill's theorisation of the functioning of human rights does not stop here. He also draws broader conclusions about the consequences of this shift for the global society. These conclusions are very important for a full understanding of his position as well as for our analysis of the sociology of human rights and our approach to human rights as a mechanism with a particular way to function. The most striking thesis he advances relates to the disappearance of the distinction between the legal system and the political system.[129] This is surprising against the backdrop of his claim to construct an explanation of the constitutional form in contemporary society on the basis of society's demand for inclusion, as articulated by Luhmann,[130] and his general reliance on the idea of functional differentiation.[131]

As we have seen, for Luhmann, the legal and the political systems in a functionally differentiated society are clearly distinguishable due to their

is understood to encompass these latest functional developments highlighted by Thornhill through the term 'transnational rights'.

125 See e.g. Ibid., 4–5, 19.

126 Ibid., 23. These two aspects: exclusionary function of fundamental rights and their role in enhancing the power of states occupies more prominent role in Thornhill's discussions of domestic constitutional experience in Thornhill, *Constitutions*.

127 For a shorter version of this argument see Thornhill, 'Rights and Constituent Power'. However, a detailed justification and development of the argument is contained in Thornhill, *Transnational Constitutions*.

128 Thornhill, *Transnational Constitutions*, 100–101.

129 Ibid., Chapter 7.

130 Ibid., 9.

131 Ibid., 13.

different functions and different codes. Precisely because these two systems are constituted as separate systems, they entertain a very close relationship and are interconnected in complex ways. The most important concept that helps Luhmann to articulate the links between the legal and the political system is the concept of structural coupling, which is exemplified by the constitution or more precisely within the traditional domestic context by the constitutional state. If Thornhill's diagnosis is correct, and the legal and the political systems become conflated and form one single system, it means that social differentiation is in regress and the de-differentiation of society that fundamental rights were supposed to prevent is taking place. For Luhmann, this is not a celebratory but rather a dangerous development in a sense that the social system becomes less complex and therefore can resolve fewer problems and respond to fewer demands.[132] Equally important is the idea that one single system performs one particular function or set of functions that are distinct from those of other systems.[133] If the legal and the political system become one, they do fulfil a function distinct from the sum of functions of the political and the legal system when they were separate. This function would need to be articulated clearly, which is not yet the case in the present state of Thornhill's scholarship, but most importantly it might mean that we live in a world where no system is dedicated to 'das Bereithalten der Kapazität zu kolektiv bindendem Entscheiden' [keeping ready the capacity for collective binding decision-making],[134] and no system stabilises normative expectations over time.[135] Thornhill does say that this merger of law and politics results in 'abstracting of a general system of inclusion'.[136] However, this does not answer the question about the function of this system of inclusion: inclusion in what, for what purposes, according to what binary code, etc. The ambiguity of Thornhill's position could also be illustrated by the following statement:

[132] 'Es ist eine gesunde wissenschaftliche Hypothese zu vermuten, daβ differenzierte Sozialordnungen das Problem des menschlichen Daseins in der Welt wirksamer zu lösen vermögen als undifferenzierte Sozialordnungen. Und wenn die Differenzierung in dem gegenwärtig erreichten Ausmasse erhalten werden soll, sind Grundrechte – oder bisher unentdeckte funktionale Äquivalente – vonnöten.' Luhmann, *Grundrechte*, 198.

[133] Luhmann, *Politik*, 76–77. [134] Luhmann, *Politik*, 84. Author's translation.

[135] Luhmann, *Law*, 147–148, more specifically using Luhmann's words: 'Abstractly, law deals with the social cost of the time binding of expectations. Concretely, law deals with the function of the stabilization of normative expectations by regulating how they are generalized in relation to their temporal, factual, and social dimensions.'

[136] Thornhill, *Transnational Constitutions*, 368.

> Transnational rights allow society to absorb or to insulate itself against the highly acentric demands for legislation which it creates, and they establish an inclusionary structure in which society can preserve the elemental form of a political system and create clearly legitimated laws ...[137]

This statement does affirm that the political system still exists, which seems contradictory to the affirmation that 'contemporary society has lost, or is losing, the essential distinction between the legal system and the political system'.[138] Some of this ambiguity can be easily overcome if we return to Luhmann's terminology and reformulate this inclusionary structure as the gradual development and complexification of the structural coupling between the global legal and the global political systems, the existence of which Luhmann, as was mentioned previously, denied.[139] Luhmann himself highlighted the difficulty of articulating the relationship between the two systems. Nevertheless, despite all the complexity of interactions between these two systems he insisted that they are not deprived of their separate existence. Rather, this called for 'more specific forms of description'.[140] However, if it is true that the global legal and the global political systems merge, then we could affirm that human rights instead of supporting functional differentiation of the global society act in the opposite direction and lead to a dedifferentiation of the global society.

If we regard Thornhill's diagnosis of the functioning of human rights within the global society on its own, the powerful insight it provides poses one fundamental dilemma from the perspective of the functional differentiation theory. The growing significance of human rights as mechanisms of inclusion and legitimation is accompanied, according to Thornhill, by two complementary developments: severance of the inclusionary and legitimating basis in the people (or constituent power) and growing significance of courts and quasi-judicial bodies as sites of articulation of rights that then serve as inclusionary mechanisms. Or to put it differently using Thornhill's terminology: the conceptual basis of legitimacy is displaced from constituent power to human rights and the practice of constitutional legitimation is transferred from legislature to courts.[141] This relocation of the practice of constitutional legitimation from however imperfect democratic bodies to elitist institutions raises a question of democracy. In terms of functional differentiation theory, historically, democracy marked a shift from a stratified society to a functionally differentiated and thus more

[137] Ibid., 383. [138] Ibid., 367. [139] See text at note 110. [140] Luhmann, *Law*, 373.
[141] Thornhill, *Transnational Constitutions*, 100.

inclusive and egalitarian society with an opening up of politics to wider populations.[142] If now the practice of constitutional legitimation is transferred to an elitist non-democratic body, this might signify the return to a stratified society. Obviously stratification will operate differently under conditions of globalisation, but nevertheless it would mark a turn away from functionally differentiated society and a return to a stratified society.

Thus, Thornhill's analysis poses two fundamental dilemmas: in relation to his thesis about the merge of the legal and the political systems, beyond the danger of de-differentiation, it actually questions the role of human rights as mechanisms situated at the continuum of fundamental rights in domestic systems. Fundamental rights in domestic systems function as devices preventing de-differentiation. If human rights as inclusionary mechanisms lead to a less differentiated society, they function differently; they do not function as de-differentiation mechanisms (fundamental rights). Secondly, if the inclusionary system of the contemporary global society based on human rights displaces the practice of constitutional legitimation from democratic institutions into elitist institutions (such as court, tribunals and quasi-judicial bodies) this can mark a return to a stratified society with less equality that stands in contradiction to the goals of constitutionalism understood broadly (as articulated in Chapter 1). Since this is due to the role of human rights, we cannot affirm, as the dominant scholarship does, that human rights are part and parcel of global constitutionalism. This also marks the need for an alternative to human rights within the project of constitutionalisation of international law or, as Luhmann puts it, for a functional equivalent. The search for alternatives forms the core of the next chapter.

c) Teubner and Constitutionalisation without Politics

Teubner's fundamental idea that distinguishes his position from Luhmann's relates to the thesis that constitutions can emerge as a result of functional differentiation and specialisation within any subsystem of society, not only as a structural coupling between the legal and the political system.[143] Since we did not discuss Teubner's views on constitution and fundamental rights in relation to domestic contexts,[144] his general

[142] Luhmann, *Politik*, 96–97. [143] Teubner, *Constitutional Fragments*, 3–4.

[144] This is due to the fact that Teubner does not articulate his theory at two levels as Thornhill does. He addresses his constitutional questions immediately at the global level.

views on constitution and constitutionalisation will be presented first, before discussing his articulation of the human rights mechanism.

Although Teubner does not articulate a clear picture of his general views on constitution and fundamental rights within domestic contexts as Thornhill, he does formulate a few general remarks that enhance understanding of his view of constitutionalism. He mentions the following elements (or their sustainable analogies) that a particular functional system needs to exhibit in order to be able to have a constitution: the nation-state *pouvoir constituant*; the self-constitution of a collective; democratic decision-making; and the organisational part of a political constitution in the strict sense.[145] According to Teubner, every constitution has a double function that distinguishes it from simple legislation: to constitute political power (autonomisation of political power from other types of power) and limit it (through protection of individual spheres of autonomy).[146] When describing constitutionalisation within a functional framework, he emphasises constitutions as the self-identity or self-description of a system, which he distinguishes from a formal organisation of a particular regime.[147] Here it is important to highlight the similarity between the views of Thornhill and Teubner.[148] In describing the function of constitutions, they highlight their constitutive function in a sense of the autonomisation of politics (or other social systems in Teubner's case). In this they depart from Luhmann's emphasis on the role of constitutions as a structural coupling between law and politics. According to Luhmann a system can be autonomous in the sense of the operatively closed meaning that 'the autopoiesis of the system can be performed only with the system's own operations'[149] while not necessarily yet structurally coupled. Obviously such an autonomous system without structural couplings would not be able to sustain itself for a very long time, but from Luhmann's point of view it is important to distinguish the process of autonomisation of the system from the process of structural coupling. A structural coupling exemplifies the capacity of

145 Teubner, *Constitutional Fragments*, 8.

146 Ibid., 17. He speaks of power, as this is the traditional medium addressed by constitutions within the framework of states. When extending his constitutional thoughts to the global arena and constitutionalisation of functional systems, power will be replaced by the equivalent medium of each system (e.g. money for economics, knowledge for science).

147 Ibid., 66 in particular, but see also broadly 61–72.

148 Ibid., 75. Interestingly, when discussing constitutional function as constitutive/limitative, Teubner quotes Thornhill, not Luhmann.

149 Luhmann, *Law*, 381.

the system to communicate with its environment. While exclusion/inclusion and constant 'protection' of the system to maintain its integrity are important in structural couplings, their rationality cannot be fully understood without remembering that they are created to entertain the relationship between a system and its environment.

In relation to the global realm, Teubner supports the view of Luhmann – disputed by Thornhill – that the structural coupling between law and politics does not exist at the level of world society.[150] Thus he states, 'Yet the triangular constellation of politics-law-subsystem which . . . bore the societal sub-constitutions in the nation state, has no counterpart in the global context.'[151] The political system of the world society does not have a comprehensive constitution; it only developed constitutional fragments for particular subareas.[152] Thus, we are faced with a strange phenomenon: 'the self-constitutionalization of global orders without a state'.[153] According to Thornhill this is not at all strange because the constitution is not tied to the state form but to the political system and as the political system evolves, the constitution evolves and detaches itself from the state form. However, for Teubner this is a strange phenomenon because according to him what is constitutionalised is not the political system of the global society but its various functional systems, or more precisely social processes 'beneath' the function systems such as formal organisations or contractual arrangements.[154] However, transnational regimes[155] as vectors of constitutionalisation processes become a normal phenomenon for Teubner once the key of any constitutional process is redefined as self-identity and self-description of any functional system, not as a structural coupling between law and politics.

Within the context of this vision of constitutions as emerging in relation to transnational regimes, the task for human rights is redefined: 'one cannot regard the horizontal effect of fundamental rights as purely a problem of power. This would miss its real task: *to limit expansionist tendencies of social subsystems* that do not function through the medium of power.'[156] When discussing human rights, Teubner starts from the premise that it is not possible to deny 'the worldwide validity, higher right and constitutional rank of universal human rights'.[157] This is very much in line with the mainstream constitutionalist literature and, as this book

[150] Teubner, *Constitutional Fragments*, 52. [151] Ibid., 44. [152] Ibid., 52.
[153] Ibid., 53. [154] Ibid., 54–55.
[155] Defined as a 'set of principles, norms, rules, and decision-making procedures around which actors' expectations converge in a given cause-area', Ibid., 58, footnote omitted.
[156] Ibid., 12 (emphasis added). [157] Ibid., 125.

argues, needs to be supported by stronger evidence than is currently available.

Similarly to Thornhill, Teubner highlights the exclusion/inclusion dynamic in human rights as central to their role in social systems.[158] However, if previously constitutions were centred around individual/state (power) dynamic, within the context of global functional systems with the differentiation of various spheres (medicine, knowledge, education, etc.), each system needs to be restricted through human rights to protect individuals from the expansionist dynamics of each specific medium.[159] However, Teubner does not only displace constitutions and with them human rights from state context to the context of transnational regimes, he also radically redefines the direction of human rights in the following sense. In the traditional understanding of human rights as extensions of fundamental rights, they are aimed at protecting individuals. Teubner redirects human rights to also protect institutions.[160] This is justified by the fact that autonomous communicative matrices (like discourses or systems) endanger the integrity not only of individuals, but also of institutions and other persons.[161] Taking into account this particular danger as coming from autonomous communicative matrices, even in relation to individuals, human rights require redefinition: the 'human rights question should be understood as people being threatened not by their fellows, but by anonymous communicative processes'.[162] This obviously raises a series of difficult questions in relation to the implementation and practice of human rights.[163] In his attempt to tackle these difficulties, Teubner concludes that 'the justice of human rights can, then, at best be formulated negatively. It is aimed at removing unjust situations, not creating just ones.'[164] Therefore, human rights in Teubner's reading are also limited to their negative aspect.

Finally, it is worth mentioning that Teubner supports the idea that constitutionalisation needs to be accompanied by a strengthening of democracy.[165] The strengthening of democracy should be achieved not through institutions but by strengthening the democratic potential of civil society itself.[166] The inclusionary effect of human rights, according to Teubner, is a way of achieving this. In this regard, Teubner's view

158 Ibid., 132–134. 159 Ibid., 139–142.

160 This (institutional rights) is mentioned as one of the three dimensions of fundamental rights alongside personal and properly human rights. Ibid., 145. For the purposes of our analysis we do not need to go into details of these dimensions. Signalling the existence of institutional rights is however crucial.

161 Ibid., 143. 162 Ibid., 144. 163 These are discussed at ibid., 146–149.

164 Ibid., 149. 165 Ibid., 138–139. 166 Ibid., 134.

of human rights contradicts to some extent Thornhill's diagnosis of constitutionalism and especially of human rights at the global level. The main point of discord resides in the significant role attributed to courts and tribunals by Thornhill, which, as discussed above, undermines the democratic potential, whereas for Teubner this democratic potential is strengthened by the use of human rights.

3 *(Un)certainties of Human Rights Functioning*

This section started with the aim of discovering the functioning of human rights at the global level and comparing it to the functioning of fundamental rights at the domestic level. Within the tradition of functional differentiation based on systems theory that was used here to elucidate the functioning of human rights, there was a lot of ambiguity surrounding this issue. It was clear for Luhmann that human rights function differently and cannot be equated to fundamental rights in domestic constitutions. In one of his works first published in German in 1993, he even denied the very existence of a constitution at the global level, although he affirmed the existence of both the global political and the global legal systems.[167] Luhmann's perspective on the possible developments of the global system and its subsystems was not firmly set. However, apart from the possibility that the global society will develop mechanisms similar to those we know from his analysis as applied to states, Luhmann equally seriously contemplated the possibility that the global system might develop a mechanism unknown from our historical domestic experience, including the disappearance of the need for law. Luhmann's analysis indicated two major impediments to the constitutional developments at the global level: differentiation in states and the exclusion/inclusion dynamic that produces extreme consequences at the global level. Two theorists expanded Luhmann's theory and provided a more detailed articulation of the functioning of human rights at the global level.

The most important innovation to the system theoretical functional differentiation framework as articulated by Luhmann and introduced by Teubner is the idea of constitutions as being detached from political power. According to Teubner constitutions are emerging within different global functional systems without any relationship to politics. If we use

[167] The reference is here to the first German edition of Luhamnn, *Law*, as discussed in section 'Maintaining a Global Normative System'.

the language of Luhmann, we could describe what Teubner proposes as structural couplings between law and each global functional system. While the idea that global functional systems after having differentiated themselves would need to be able to communicate with their environment (of which law is one very important component) is perfectly plausible, the question of whether these structural couplings can be called a constitution is highly debatable. As Thornhill's position demonstrates, it is equally plausible to define a constitution first and foremost through its link to politics. In this case the process described by Teubner cannot properly be called constitutional. This in turn again raises the question of the functioning of human rights at the global level. If we return to Teubner's framework, once the constitutional quality of these processes taking place between law and various transnational regimes is questioned, it is no longer possible to even remotely associate the functioning of human rights at the global level with the operation of fundamental rights within the constitutional tradition of nation-states.

Another important difference between the views of the two authors relates to the legitimation function of human rights at the global level. If for Thornhill human rights clearly displace constituent power as a legitimating mechanism, simultaneously displacing the arena of legitimation from democratic bodies to courts, we can infer from Teubner's analysis that for him, human rights support democratisation and thus legitimation through a more traditional mechanism and within a more traditional arena (civil society). The conclusions we can draw from the analysis by these two authors are threefold: first, there is still a lot of uncertainty surrounding the role and functioning of human rights at the global level. Second, whatever the function one ascribes to human rights, it is neither the traditionally conceived protection of individuals against states nor a functioning comparable to the function of fundamental rights in domestic systems. Third and most importantly, for both authors human rights represent a mechanism of inclusion. The authors diverge on how, whom and what human rights include, by the dynamic of inclusion emerges as a fundamental feature of the human rights mechanism. Inclusion always presupposes and has as its corollary exclusion and thus arbitrariness. Therefore, human rights participates in the maintenance of mechanisms described in Chapter 1 that stand in contradiction to global constitutionalism's aims. I discuss the consequences following from these findings for the broader question of the relationship between human rights and global constitutionalism in the concluding part of this chapter.

E Conclusions

This chapter's main aim was to examine the functioning of human rights at the global level in order to assess the thesis advanced by proponents of international constitutionalism according to which human rights constitute a cornerstone of the international constitutional order through fulfilment of functions similar to fundamental rights in domestic constitutional contexts. The analysis performed on the basis of sociological system theory led us to question the adequacy, efficiency and necessity of an approach associating international human rights with national constitutional guarantees. The main argument developed is the following: while human rights and national constitutional rights do at times fulfil the same or similar functions, they do not function in the same way. Therefore, using one to theorise, develop or elucidate the other can create distortions and hide the functioning of the other mechanism. For example, in relation to both fundamental rights and international human rights, several authors highlighted, although to different degrees, the inclusionary function. However, in order to efficiently fulfil this inclusionary function, different mechanisms are used within the context of fundamental rights, as opposed to international human rights. The best illustration of this point is the fact that fundamental rights fulfil their function at the domestic level as part of the constitution, which is a structural coupling between the legal and the political system. At the international or global level, authors either deny the existence of the structural coupling between the legal and the political systems in the form of a constitution (Luhmann and Teubner) or, when affirming the existence of a constitution at the global level, they have to admit the displacement of the function of human rights to a different area (Thornhill). In both cases there is a clear difference in the way human rights fulfil their function as compared to fundamental rights.

Advocates of international constitutionalism who agree that international human rights are comparable and should be modelled upon national constitutional rights because they fulfil the same function commit a mistake. They disregard the fact that the mechanism that allows international human rights to fulfil a function similar to that of national constitutional rights is different. To put it more clearly: we can imagine the existence of two systems within which similar functions are fulfilled by two mechanisms functioning differently. If we attempt to restructure one of the systems using the other as a model because we believe that this other system fulfils the function more efficiently, we might completely destroy the first system because we do not pay attention to the way the system functions as a whole. By making some adjustments only in relation to the mechanism that fulfils the particular function, we distort the entire system that will perhaps at the end have no mechanism at all to fulfil the function we wanted to fix or improve.

Beyond the simple questioning of the parallelism between fundamental rights and human rights, the analysis performed in this chapter has a broader significance for this study. Firstly, it sheds new light on the role human rights play in constructing paradigms central to the current state of theorising in international constitutionalism. Secondly, the analysis itself allows comprehending human rights from a perspective so far unexplored in the debates on global constitutionalism. Before considering these two aspects, it needs to be emphasised that so far a fundamental ambiguity surrounds the functioning of human rights at the global level. Therefore, some of the propositions advanced will necessarily be only tentative and provisional. However, the functioning of human rights as inclusionary mechanisms emerges as a common denominator. Although, as already stated, the particulars of human rights as an inclusionary mechanism are assessed differently by different authors. Therefore, human rights as an inclusionary mechanism necessarily create and make invisible the exclusion and arbitrariness that are antithetical to the goals of global constitutionalism.

In relation to the position of the individual, we can note the following. Within the tradition of global constitutionalism, the language of human rights facilitates the placing of the individual at the centre. However, the above analysis of the functioning of human rights shows a different picture. While human rights are directed at painting a particular vision of the individual, their primary concern is not the individual but the functioning of social systems. In Luhmann's vision, an individual is clearly just one of the social systems. Other authors are not that explicit on this point, but for instance, in Teubner's analysis an individual is just one of the objects of protection of human rights alongside institutions. Therefore, we can also affirm that human rights is not the best mechanism to be used for the promotion of a more active direct role of individuals at the global level that could lead to a paradigm shift.

Human rights, at least in Thornhill's and less explicitly in Luhmann's view, play a significant role in maintaining and re-enforcing the state and the vision of the political that allows the survival of the state. In Teubner's view, since he contests the need for the political and argues for constitutionalisation of different social subsystems at the global level, this function of human rights is less obvious. However, as discussed in the previous chapter, the state thinking still permeates Teubner's vision. Moreover, if we understand that the political emerges whenever some type of community dynamic is being formed, it is a bit strange that Teubner can present transnational functional regimes as being apolitical or affirm a constitutionalisation dynamic in absence of politics.

Thus, despite the ambiguities surrounding the precise understanding of the functioning of human rights at the global level, we can clearly discern the tendency of human rights to serve the state and the political with its exclusion/inclusion dynamic in allowing them to adapt to the evolving realities of the global. Individuals again emerge as an element among others that is used to maintain the existing paradigms. Simultaneously, the ambiguity and uncertainty of the current state of human rights opens up possibilities for imagining alternatives, including those without the state. This is what was indicated by Luhmann and attempted by Teubner. However, taking into account our critical remarks on the framework proposed by Teubner, rethinking the existing paradigms and the future of global constitutionalism depends also on the rethinking of human rights, on finding an alternative to the imagery of human rights. This is attempted in the next chapter.

3

The Other of Human Rights and Global Constitutionalism

The analysis of the previous chapter has demonstrated several shortcomings of the current discourse on global constitutionalism and ordering at the global level as it relates to human rights. Therefore, the need for alternatives has become apparent. However, if the study remains within the tradition of international law as inspired by Western experiences of nation-state building, any proposed alternatives will remain vulnerable to criticism that is usually directed at this tradition. In addition, any alternatives that come from within the same discipline that produced the discourse on international constitutionalism will be able to provide only partial answers and will be of limited usefulness and novelty. Therefore, in this chapter the study turns to two traditions with the hope of uncovering some new potential for thinking about power in global ordering from the perspective of aims traditionally pursued by global constitutionalism. One of these traditions goes beyond law, another beyond the West.

Ancient Greece is an example of a non-legal ordering. This statement requires a few clarifications. 'Ancient Greece' is a very vague term. It refers to divers traditions both spatially and temporally. Over the span of several centuries, regulation of social ordering in some Greek city-states developed into a legal system, albeit in a nascent form. Although no ancient Greek legal order acquired the same level of systematisation as Roman law, it is still possible to say that at some point in time a legal system existed in several Greek city-states. The focus of this chapter will be on developments that took place before it became possible to compare social ordering of Greek city-states to modern legal systems. It will also take into account scholarly debates over the meaning and functioning of various terms and notions that challenge the conventional understanding of the ancient Greek regulations as 'legal'. Geographically, the main focus will be on Athens. Generally, the focus on ancient Greece is also determined by its symbolic importance to the modern constitutional developments in the West. However, as we will see, many of the analogies drawn between modern constitutional experience and ancient Greek political practices are based on projections of our modern understandings into the ancient Greek context.

Islam is an example of a non-Western legal or, more precisely, normative order. Similarly to ancient Greece, Islam is a very multifaceted phenomenon that covers several centuries and divers geographical regions. The approach adopted in this chapter focuses on the historical experience of attempts to regulate and theorise the regulation of the exercise of power before Western legal thought left its imprint on Islamic normative tradition. The substantive reasons for selecting Islam will become clear in due course. At this stage suffice it to say that Islam is often viewed in opposition to the Western legal tradition, therefore contrasting these two apparently opposed orders offers more radical insights.

A Before the Law: Controlling Power in Ancient Greece

1 From Community to Individual in Ancient Greece

As the birthplace of democracy, ancient Greece occupies a highly symbolic place in modern constitutional thought. However, many discussions of ancient Greek tradition in constitutional writings are brief and confined to a few main themes. These discussions mostly focus on the period of the height of Athenian democracy, mainly fifth century BC and after. This chapter will take a different approach. In order to discover new mechanisms and new ways of ensuring the control of power and protection of individuals but also to understand the key elements that allowed the establishment of Athenian democracy, the chapter will discuss the development of legal and normative ideas leading to the establishment of Athenian democracy without focusing on this democracy as such. The main goal is to understand mechanisms and shifts in ideas that allowed the establishment of Athenian democracy, i.e. how the mechanism was built.

Ancient Greek culture is separated from us by time and language. Despite the rich amount of information we possess about ancient Greece compared to other ancient civilisations, access to a full understanding is complicated by our fragmented knowledge of the lives of ancient Greek communities. In addition, the language of ancient Greece is unfamiliar to the majority of international lawyers and also different from the modern Greek language. Therefore, even if we are used to translating certain words in a certain way into English, by attributing to these ancient Greek terms the modern meaning of English words, we often lose the grasp of what these words meant to ancient Greek people. For example, we are accustomed to translate *nómos* as 'law' and *dike* as 'justice'. But do these English terms really convey what ancient Greek people expressed when talking about *nómos* or *dike* at different times in ancient Greek history? The investigations on this topic performed by historians and philologists indicate that it is not possible to subsume these ancient Greek terms under modern English words. This is all the more obvious when taking into account that legal phenomenon was still developing at the time of ancient Greek civilisation. It could not have the meaning of fully established and formed legal notions. Therefore, in what follows, the idea of law and justice as it developed in ancient Greece is traced based on existing historical and philological studies. The emphasis is on mechanisms that were put in place at that time to ensure absence of arbitrariness and control of power, not on specific rules.

One initial observation is warranted. The classical Greek language does not have a specific term for 'right' in the sense of individual rights, human rights, etc., which is an indispensable part of modern constitutional and human rights thinking. This does not necessarily mean that Greeks did not have or did not know the concept of rights as such. However, the absence of a specific term indicates that even if the concept of rights appeared in the ancient Greek legal culture, it was a new concept that did not exist from the beginning of emergence of the ancient Greek legal and normative culture. This fact is also important in highlighting some fundamental differences in the ways that power was controlled and regulated in ancient Greece as opposed to in modern nation-states and international law.

If we attempt to understand the emergence and functioning of the idea of law in ancient Greece, at least the three following concepts need to be understood: *themis, dike* and *nómos*. These concepts are linked and partially overlapping. Taken together they indicate the changes through which ancient Greek society went to arrive at a concept or idea of law that shaped the classical Athenian democracy so much praised by modern constitutionalists.

Nómos is not the first term to be used by ancient Greeks to speak about the order or custom that governs a particular community. According to a very detailed study of the Greek root that is at the origin of the term *nómos*, namely the root *nem-*, by Emmanuel Laroche, Homer's poems, the earliest ancient Greek text that can be used to study ancient Greece, do not contain this term.[1] However, Homer does use multiple times the verb of the same root.[2] As soon as the presence and use of the term *nómos* can be attested in ancient Greek sources – around eighth century BC – the term already has a variety of meanings.[3] Without considering the richness of all the connotations and meanings of the term *nómos*, including in their historical development, it is not possible to fully comprehend the place and role of normativity in ancient Greek tradition, including as expressed through the term *nómos*, which is so easily translated today as 'law'. We will return to these various meanings of *nómos* after discussing other terms that have normative connotations before the clear emergence of *nómos* as the dominant term associated with the legal.

In the Homeric poetry there are other terms that indicate commonly accepted practices, behaviours and ways of doing things that come closest to the modern notion of law indicating normative orientations within a particular community. These are the notions of *themis* and *dike*. We need first to understand the normative idea expressed in these earlier terms before the term *nómos* with its connotation of law became dominant.

The term *themis* is the 'word most often used in the Iliad and the Odyssey that tends to be translated with legislative overtones'.[4] However, it is not possible to equate this to the modern understanding of law. Firstly, *themis* has strong links to the will of gods. It can be argued that *themis* is created by the will of gods.[5] The will of gods becomes known to humans through pronouncements. Those who can pronounce the will of gods in the ancient Greek society are first kings, later broader nobility – both of

[1] Laroche, *L'Histoire*, 164. There exists one particular place in Homer where initially there was a discussion about the potential presence of the term *nómos* (Homer, Odysseus, Book 1, Verse 3). However, all or at least the majority of authors abandoned the version with the term *nómos*. See e.g. Ostwald, who researched extensively on the term *nómos* and stated that Hesiod, not Homer is the first to use the term *nómos* (Ostwald, *Nomos*, 21). The relevant word reads as *νόον*, not *νόμον*. It is important to note that in the widely known (among international lawyers) treatise by Schmitt, *The Nomos of the Earth*, Schmitt constructs one of his arguments supporting his interpretation of *nómos* that is then used to present a particular vision of international law based on the reading of this verse from Homer as containing the term *nómos*. There is no justification for this choice except Schmitt's own preference. (Ibid., 76) He simply abandons the standard reading justified by philologists and historians to create his own argument.

[2] Laroche, *L'Histoire*, 7–13. These meanings will be considered in more detail below, when the term *nómos* is discussed.

[3] Ibid., 166. [4] Stratton, 'Writing and Law', 106. [5] Ehrenberg, *Rechtsidee*, 6.

whom traced their origins to gods – and finally judges, when judges appear as actors different from kings and noblemen. Therefore, at these earlier stages *themis* can be understood as a judging act, namely as a decision based on the order within a particular society and that simultaneously maintained this order.[6] At later stages *themis* acquires the meaning of societal norm in a sense of what is appropriate or convenient in a particular society without it becoming law. According to Ehrenberg, this obedience to gods' commands creates necessary conditions for the later emerging of norms created by a particular community and respected by members of this community:[7] 'Aus der Unterwerfung unter die gemeinsame göttliche Autorität erwächst der Gehorsam gegen einen Willen der Gemeinschaft.'[8] Thus, *themis* carries with it the notion of authority that is necessary for the later creation of notions more closely related to the modern idea of law. Finally, it is also important to highlight that the main reason for the demise of *themis* is its incapacity to create a space for contestation and expression of opinions by wider layers of the population.[9] This particular deficiency of *themis* led to the rise in the prominence of the term *dike*.

Dike is usually translated as justice. However, its meaning is more complex. According to Laroche initially, especially in the Homeric epic, *themis* and *dike* often converge.[10] According to him, they developed distinct meanings only later.[11] Ehrenberg demonstrates that *dike* is something that ends the quarrel, replacing violence, and therefore is better understood as right distribution.[12] In this sense *dike* can be associated with law not in a technical modern sense but as a mechanism to put things right (*Recht, droit*). However, *dike* needs to be distinguished from the concept of a legal norm. *Dike* is subjective in the sense that it represents the right outcome of a dispute, the right judgment for a particular case, while a legal norm is by its nature objective in the sense that it applies to all cases that it intends to regulate. Gagarin convincingly demonstrates that in Homeric texts *dike* reveals two areas of usage: one is '"characteristic or characteristic behavior" with a suggestion of "proper behavior"'[13] always referring to a group of persons.[14] The second meaning, which then became dominant for several centuries, corresponds to the ideas advanced by other authors, namely a process for the peaceful settlement of disputes.[15] Within this second meaning all authors emphasise the orientation towards community's well-being when seeking a

6 Stratton, 'Writing and Law', 107. 7 Ehrenberg, *Rechtsidee*, 50–52. 8 Ibid., 50.
9 Ibid., 52. 10 Laroche, *L'Histoire*, 164. 11 Ibid. 12 Ehrenberg, *Rechtsidee*, 63–64.
13 Gagarin, 'Works and Days', 83. 14 Ibid., 82.
15 Ibid., 81; see also Gagarin, 'Archaic Thought' in general.

solution for a particular dispute, finding a compromise between disputing parties so that the peace within a community can be re-established and maintained. Gagarin emphasises economic and property aspects in particular.[16] However, whatever the area of application of the idea of *dike*, it is important to highlight the absence of moral overtones and connotations in this term in ancient Greek thought during the period that interests us here.

During this period *dike*, similarly to *themis*, maintains its relationship to the divine.[17] Even judgments made technically by human beings (for instance, kings) are said to be divine judgments if they re-establish equilibrium, if they are 'right' judgments.[18] Thus, both *dike* and *themis* can be described as religious and empirical notions of the order of things and ways of doing within particular communities that allow these communities to be peaceful and prosperous. However, *dike* has an additional layer of meaning that is not contained in the *themis*. As stated above, *themis*, even when it acquires the meaning of a societal norm – what is appropriate in a particular society – is nevertheless based on the superiority of nobility and respect for nobility. The promise of the right decision that *dike* carries with itself is addressed equally to everybody: king, noble or craftsman. Therefore, *dike* becomes the way the lower classes of Greek society claim justice, and thus becomes a basis for the worldview encompassing all human beings independently of their wealth and nobility status.[19] Through this inclusion of all human beings a sense of community is also constituted. However, it would be wrong to read this as a one-way process. Ehrenberg demonstrates how the notion of *dike* simultaneously empowered individuals (especially the lower class) and reinforced the sense of community by protecting it against the threats coming from too strong individualisation, including will to power or nonconformity by particularly strong individuals who would then attempt to impose their will on the community.

Within the move from *themis* to *dike* in the ancient Greece, a movement from a status-based society to a community-based society can be observed. If *themis* as a societal order comes from above, independently

[16] This is his overall argument in both articles mentioned above. Similarly, see Stratton, 'Writing and Law'.

[17] Gagarin, 'Archaic Thought', 193. [18] Ehrenberg, *Rechtsidee*, 63.

[19] Obviously we have always to remember the exclusion of slaves, women and other groups from active membership in ancient Greek communities. However, the argument is made here at a more abstract level to see the dynamics of concepts and their development, not to deny continuing exclusions.

of demands and needs of lower-class people, *dike* produces an order construed and sustained by all through an effort to conform to and respect the right judgment, the judgment most suitable for the prosperity of all as a community. This mechanism that does not yet know the idea of law in the modern sense nevertheless ensures protection against the arbitrariness of power and imposition of views and opinions by particularly powerful individuals. This opens up a way towards equality and simultaneously reinforces the sense of community. Thus the mechanism at work is put in motion by two movements: (1) recognition of the fact that everybody deserves his/her right and that they should have a way to claim this; (2) emerging understanding of the group of people living together as a community and not simply the ruling (nobility) and the ruled. It is remarkable how the notion of *dike* accomplishes this double movement of community creation and empowerment of individuals without making recourse to the notion of law: everybody has a claim to get a 'right' decision, to get a situation 'straight'. This creates a sense of community and belonging. What community? How is it defined? Different authors offer divergent views in this regard. For some, the community in question can only be a quite homogeneous and thus spatially limited community. For others it can encompass the whole world. However, once it is emerging, the community has claims on its own and uses the notion of *dike* to prevent extreme individualism and usurpation of power (e.g. tyranny).

The concept of *nómos* develops later than *themis* and *dike*. Various ancient Greek authors use *nómos* to express several ideas that although linked, lead into different directions. For example, Martin Ostwald identifies at least ten different meanings or connotations of *nómos* in an article[20] and thirteen meanings in his book on *nómos*.[21] Laroche, in the chapter dedicated to *nómos* in his book, also emphasises the multiplicity of meanings of *nómos* in areas ranging from music to politics, as well as the simultaneity of the emergence of these different meanings.[22] In this regard Ostwald also stressed that for any Greek using the term *nómos* 'in some specific context, he cannot have wanted to stress only one of its many nuances to the exclusion of all others'.[23] In our effort to understand the ancient Greek concept of law, we should always remain acutely aware of the fact that words carry with them many connotations and nuances and that all are equally important to what 'law' meant to ancient Greeks.

[20] Ostwald, 'Pindar', 120–126. [21] Ostwald, *Nomos*, 20–54.
[22] Laroche, *L'Histoire*, 166. [23] Ostwald, 'Pindar', 126.

However, not all these meanings and connotations existed at all times when a particular term is used. For example, it is attested by several researchers that the meaning of *nómos* as a written law (collection of rules for general application) is one of the latest meanings of *nómos*.[24] Thus, it is also important to remain aware of the temporal aspect. This being said, we still do not have a better way of approaching *nómos* than through an artificial separation of its different connotations as they developed over time and by explaining them with terms familiar to a contemporary reader.

A very detailed and widely cited study by Laroche carefully traces the origin of *nómos* to the verb *nemo*. This verb has also a rich variety of meanings and connotations that changed over time.[25] For our purposes, it is important to emphasise that from the beginning this verb means 'distribute', or 'attribute', including distribution of destiny by Gods.[26] Laroche keenly emphasises that 'distribution' in the sense that the verb denotes is not equivalent and shall not be confused with partition. Firstly, because the act of partition is always denoted by other verbs.[27] Secondly, the verb *nemo* is often used to denote the distribution of destiny by gods. In this context it would be absurd to talk about any partition, because only something that has limits can be partitioned, but gods' power and destiny are limitless: 'la Fortune est infinie comme la toute-puissance divine elle-meme.'[28] Other early meanings of the verb include 'graze'; 'inhabit', 'live' (speaking of humans); and 'govern', 'administer'.

Once the noun *nómos* appears in the available Greek sources, it carries with it a richness of connotations, although the meaning of *nómos* as a written set of rules of general application is clearly a later phenomenon as stated above.[29] It is important to emphasise that even when the understanding of *nómos* as written law emerged, initially, it was not dominant.

[24] For instance, such authors as Ehrenberg, Heinimann and Vlastos confirm that the emergence of *nómos* as positive law dates to the sixth century, not before: Ehrenberg, *Aspects*, 75, and Ehrenberg, *Rechtsidee*, 122; Heinimann, *Nomos und Physis*, 72; Vlastos, 'Isonomia', 349. Ostwald demonstrates that by the end of the fifth century *nómos* is firmly entrenched as an official term for 'statute'. (Ostwald, *Nomos*, viii and in general)

[25] Laroche, *L'Histoire*, 7–68. [26] Ibid., 9.

[27] Ibid. Here again we should mention that in the well-known study on international law by Schmitt (*The Nomos of the Earth*) the distinction between partition and distribution that is essential for the understanding of *nómos* is not maintained. Schmitt always attributes to the verb at the origin of term *nómos* the meaning 'division', which is incorrect because division implies partition, but distribution can be effectuated without partition. See also note 1 above.

[28] Ibid. [29] See above note 24.

It takes time and several important events in the life of the Greek community to establish this association between *nómos* and human-made written laws as the dominant understanding of *nómos*. In this development *nómos* gradually loses its relationship to the divine. Before discussing what made this shift in the meaning attributed to *nómos* possible, the variety of meanings attributed to this term prior to the shift must be briefly sketched.

In his study Laroche, when enumerating different occurrences of *nómos* before the fifth century, often has difficulty translating this word in particular contexts and has to explain its meaning. He mentions, for example, the following: 'rites', 'way of living', 'regular and necessary order', 'custom or practice', 'principles of social morality', 'arrangement or dosage'.[30] Ostwald, focusing on political meanings of *nómos* as they occur in different contexts before the end of the fifth century, identifies a common, underlying idea that unities all different usages of *nómos*: 'an order of some kind, which differs from other words for "order" . . . in the connotation that this order is or ought to be regarded as valid and binding by those who live under it.'[31] Thus, *nómos* is both descriptive and prescriptive, or more precisely prescriptive and descriptive meanings in earlier uses of *nómos* are blurred: fact and value coincide.[32]

The shift in the understanding of *nómos* happens during the fifth century BC. As demonstrated by Christian Meier, *nómos* from signifying something given (*gegebenes*) shifts into available, at the disposal of individual human beings (*verfügbares*) upon which humans can decide and thus change, not simply expand or add details as in previous understanding.[33] This shift is very important for the emergence of the idea that the normative order and laws are something upon which all humans can decide. On the other hand, the fact that rules and the normative are manmade makes them easier to contest and opens up the way for diversity of opinions on related matters. Simultaneously this establishes law and normative order as always fallible and imperfect.[34]

[30] Laroche, *L'Histoire*, 171–175. [31] Ostwald, *Nomos*, 20.

[32] Ibid., and Ostwald, *From Popular Sovereignty*, 86–89. [33] Meier, 'Wandel'.

[34] It is interesting to note in this regard the *nómos/physis* controversy. In itself, it is a very complex topic and outside of the framework of the present research. However, it exemplifies the shift in the understanding of *nómos* as something given and unchangeable to something that is viewed as imperfect, subject to criticism and also changeable by humans. See e.g. Heinimann, *Nomos and Physis*; for a more recent overview with further references to literature see Yoshida, *Rationality*, Chapter 7.

These developments and changes in the connotations and meanings of *nómos* should be placed side by side with other notions that influenced the development of the ancient Greek political order. For our purposes, *eunomia* and *isonomia* are particularly important. The transition from *eunomia* to *isonomia* accompanied the transition from the previous meanings of *nómos* to the understanding of *nómos* as positive law and therefore helps to comprehend the shift involved in this movement.

Eunomia denotes a good order within a given community or a community that is ordered. It is opposed at the social level to *dysnomia*: bad order or absence of order. This good order does not seem to be very precisely defined as to its substance, and it keeps a strong link to the divine order. *Eunomia* envisages the community as a potential that can realise some ideal, divine order.[35] *Eunomia* links the good order within a community to the individual behaviour of its members because good order arises as a social result of the conduct by individual members of the community.[36] The term *eunomia* features prominently at the background of Solon's reforms and his laws (adopted around 594/593 BC) that were called *thesmoi*, not *nómoi*.[37] Without going into detail of the distinction between *thesmoi* and *nómoi*, let us just remark that while *thesmos* implies an imposition of law from above and has a distinctly religious flavour, *nómos* – a word that suggests something held in common, whether a pasture or a custom – implies a law to which there is a common agreement, something that people who are subject to it themselves regard as a binding norm.[38] As the term designating written law changes from *thesmos* to *nómos*, the term *eunomia* is replaced by the term *isonomia*. The term *isonomia* is composed of two roots: *isos* (equal)[39] and *nómos*, connotations and meanings of which were described before. It is possible to affirm that at the time of the emergence of the idea of *isonomia*, it also signifies the written law/code of laws.[40]

35 Meier, 'Wandel', 11–12 highlights that *eunomia* brings realisation that a good order is possible, but this is still linked to gods. The link to gods is highlighted also in Raaflaub, 'Early Greek Thought'.

36 Lewis, *Solon*, 56–57.

37 On Solon's reforms broadly see e.g. Lewis, *Solon*; Owens, *Solon;* or Randall, *Solon*.

38 A particularly forceful argument in Ostwald, *Nomos*, in general. See also description of *nómos* as 'the most democratic word for "law" in any language' by Meiksins Wood, *Citizens to Lords*, 36.

39 The root *ισος* denotes the idea of quantitative equality in the sense of 'same', 'proportional'. See e.g. Meier, 'Wandel', 19.

40 Argument in Vlastos, 'Isonomia'.

If we remember that *isonomia* is a term meant to designate a development beyond *eunomia*, it could be translated as equality of law. According to Vlastos it can best be grasped by describing it as 'an equal share of all citizens in the control of the state'.[41] He highlights the following difference between *eunomia* and *isonomia*: the equality that is implied in the understanding of the term *isonomia* is restricted to law only, while the good order implied by the term *eunomia* covers all aspects of living together, not only law.[42] With *isonomia* and the shifting of vocabulary to designate the positive law from *thesmos* to *nómos*, the idea of order created through law agreed upon by all members of the community becomes central. In the ordering of the community the attention also shifts from a general well-being to ensuring equality in and through laws, equality in political aspects of life. Simultaneously the idea of the human being as an active agent, a creator of the order that rules the community, emerges and becomes dominant. This is accompanied by another realisation: since *nómos* is available to human beings, not given, it can also be manipulated. Therefore, human beings as free and equal individuals become the biggest adversary of *nómos* in a traditional sense but also of the social order itself and of the well-ordered society.[43] This shift to written law led to the emergence of a series of other difficulties and paradoxes related to the fact that 'laws begin to be viewed as an expression of people's absolute rights and duties (not as a protection against malfeasance)'.[44] In particular, the tension between natural law and positive law and the inability to explain the diversity of law across different communities emerge at this point, as does the distinction between real and apparent (e.g. meaning of words in laws) that leads to the emergence of legal interpretation.[45] Overall, this led to a shift away from case-by-case context-specific approach to governing the ordering in a particular community to a battle over absolute meaning and absolute truth.

Summarising the above brief presentation of various normative concepts in ancient Greek thought, we can highlight the link between the

[41] Vlastos, 'Isonomia', 352.

[42] Ibid., 352–355 emphasises that e.g. equality in land owning was dropped from reforms that postulated *isonomia* as its guiding principle (Ibid., 353); see similarly Meier, 'Wandel', 20.

[43] This idea is particularly clearly articulated in Ehrenberg, *Rechtsidee*, 139–140; but also see Ostwald. The very title of his book, *From Popular Sovereignty to the Sovereignty of Law*, highlights this idea. It should also be kept in mind that since this section represents only a summary of a very complex development, only main shifts are highlighted.

[44] Crook, 'Language', 242. [45] See ibid. in general.

stability and well-being of the community and its members as the focus of ordering central to preoccupations of ancient Greeks in times prior to the emergence of *nómos* as positive law. Equally important is the case-by-case oriented nature of dispute settlement that can be construed as the normative element of this order. The emergence of *nómos* as positive law made by members of the community reveals itself as auto-destructive device: in order to stabilise the community and to protect it and its members from tyranny and the arbitrariness of individual will, it slowly elevates and frees all individuals, thus giving them power and ability (awakening their consciousness) to act in turn and thus destroy polis: focus shifts from community to individual, thus destroying the previous mechanism. It seems, that this transition in ancient Greek thought permanently inscribes this tension between individual and law that is highlighted by Luhmann as the paradox of human rights within the political life of Western societies.

2 *From Ancient Greece to Contemporary International Law*

What can be learned from this analysis of ideas about ordering and life in common in ancient Greece for contemporary international law and its discourse of constitutionalisation? The first lesson is a reminder or another note of caution against an uncritical reliance on rights discourse as a mechanism for ensuring better life in common. We can clearly see how the individualisation and empowerment of human beings as autonomous, free and equal individuals in a society where law is understood as being at individuals' disposal creates more opportunities or even incentives for individuals to disrupt the order of life in common through pursuit of egoistic interests. We could even affirm that the happy life in common as an objective of global constitutionalism stands in contradiction with individualist orientations of human rights law.

Law as positive law that human beings make and change was a concept required at a certain point in time in order to respond to the demands of wider populations for equal inclusion into community, as compared to the previous order based on nobility supported by its claims to their divine origin. However, the mechanism inbuilt in this previous order was actually more encompassing and responsive to the complexity of life in that it embedded a structure for resolving conflicts that allowed greater flexibility and adaptability of the community in response to changing circumstances and in response to various demands. Therefore, we could describe this mechanism as a better adaptation and learning mechanism for the society as a whole. This mechanism is more cognitively oriented. If we remember that according to Luhmann perhaps today the global society is more receptive to cognitive expectations and needs mechanisms and institutions that can better respond to patterns of cognitive, not normative expectations,[46] then we can see the potential lessons that can be learned from the historical experience of ancient Greece.

Perhaps the way forward for the global society is the establishment of a mechanism allowing for case-by-case context-specific responses to arising conflicts and disagreements that are more adaptive and learn faster from these various experiences. At the same time, the discontent of wider layers of populations with elitism inbuilt into the ancient Greek order caution that such a system can only be successful if it is able to free itself from this elitism. In the contemporary global order this elitism, instead of being combated by human rights, is emerging from within human rights. Today human rights replace constituent power and shift arenas for constituent practices from democratic institutions to courts.[47] The ways to overcome this elitism are suggested based on the experience of early Islamic communities that are discussed in the next part of this chapter.

B Beyond the Law: Confronting Power in Islamic Tradition

Any human community must confront the issue of how to deal with abuses of power, how to restrain the power that some persons within the community acquire by virtue of servicing this community. Islamic tradition is no exception. Despite all the prejudices that exist today against Islam in the minds of those unfamiliar with the history of Islamic tradition, Islam also offers some valuable lessons in this area. This section focuses on the Islamic tradition of constraining and controlling power as it was articulated and discussed historically in the early days of Islam. Some later developments within this tradition will be followed, but only until the point where European powers intervened and started influencing and changing societal structures and, thus, the thinking about these issues. This focus is justified by the fact that today, Muslim majority population countries, whatever the legal framework within which they function (whether based on Islam or not), do not have to offer anything new. They simply emulate the Western tradition. The alternative

[46] See Chapter 2, section 'Luhmann and Two Ways'.

[47] See argument in Chapter 2, section 'Thornhill and the Fusion of Law and Politics'.

mechanisms that do not follow the constitutional paradigm of Western states but still achieve restraint and control of power existed in the history of Islamic societies prior to colonisation. However, these mechanisms were destroyed with the processes of colonisation, are lost today, and stand in contradiction to the modern state framework.[48]

It is also important to highlight that like many Western notions and mechanisms such as democracy, constitutionalism or human rights that are always realised in social practices only imperfectly, the mechanisms utilised by Islamic societies that will be discussed below have never been realised in an ideal and perfect form. However, this does not prevent us from studying the ideal form of these mechanisms emerging from the works of Islamic scholars and drawing lessons from the historical experience of their imperfect functioning. This part is divided in two sections similar to the previous part. The first section analyses the mechanisms of power control that were used historically within Islamic societies. The second section assesses their relevance to the modern world from the perspective of the constitutionalism's quest for controlling the power at the global level.

1 *Islam, Power and Governance: Historical Experience*

In Western academic and media discourses Islam is usually represented and studied as a religion comparable to Christianity or Judaism. Separately, and unrelated to this representation of Islam as a religious phenomenon, Islamic law is studied and discussed, often by a different group of specialists. However, in order to comprehend mechanisms used within the Islamic tradition to control and restrain power, we need to start by dismantling this separation: Islam comprehended in the West as a religion is as much 'legal' as 'Islamic law' is religious. The very idea of 'Islamic law' is an artificial intellectual creation of the West in its effort to comprehend the Islamic tradition using Western terms and concepts. This obviously does not deny the distinction that existed in the Islamic tradition between scholars and specialists in theology and 'law'.[49]

[48] For a similar argument see Hallaq, 'Muslim Rage'. See also Abou El Fadl, *Islam*; An-Na'im, 'Spirit'.

[49] On this see e.g. Johansen, *Contingency*, 3–42 where he discusses in a concise fashion the changing relationship between Islamic theology (*kalām*) and Islamic law (*fiqh*) from the first Islamic century and until the emergence of Islamic law as a discipline separate from theology, including the brief overview of the emergence of the major schools of Islamic law.

However, the term 'law' with meanings and connotations that it carries with itself is inadequate to describe the group of specialists possessing the capacity to find answers to questions of conformity to Islam and appropriate Islamic way of acting in concrete situations. This transposition of the Western political and legal experience into Islamic tradition distorted in many ways our reading of the historical experience of Islamic societies with power. In the remainder of this part the reference to 'law' and 'legal' continues to be used in its modern, Western sense. Therefore, the false dichotomy that characterises contemporary approaches to studying Islam and its ordering of society will be maintained at the linguistic level. This is justified as follows. The addressee of this work is contemporary academic audience that is mostly Western or accustomed to operate with this dichotomy in mind. Therefore, in order to make the argument comprehensible to this audience, I need to use the terminology and concepts familiar to this audience. Additionally, the dichotomy is only maintained to be deconstructed.

As perhaps many readers know, the fundamental starting point in the discussion of Islam, its contents and requirements, is the Quran, the holy book of Muslims. It is believed to be an unchanged, uncorrupted word of God. Academic study of Islamic law will raise such questions as: How much of the Quran's text deals with genuinely legal issues? How are these legal issues framed? Are they *ad hoc* responses to particular cases or general rules for universal application? Are injunctions in the Quran backed by enforcement?[50] All these questions, but especially the first one, illustrate that attempts at understanding the Quran and its normativity were undertaken from the perspective of Western experience with law and ordering of society. Some other scholars did attempt to challenge this approach.[51] In some instances, they even tried to reconstruct the functioning of Muslim communities on their own terms.[52] It is important to

[50] For some examples where this framework of analysis is obvious see: Coulson, *Introduction*, especially the discussion at 12–18. Goitein, 'The Birth-Hour'; Motzki, *Origins*; Schacht, *Introduction*.

[51] See e.g. Johansen, *Contingency*, 59, where he affirms that scholars removed those dimensions of the *fiqh* which do not enter an occidental understanding of 'law' from their legal discussion.

[52] The most prolific author in this regard is Wael B. Hallaq. His most prominent work on this issue is Hallaq, *State*. Some of the ideas expressed in this book are developed further in the form of articles. See e.g. Hallaq, 'Qur'ānic Constitutionalism' or Hallaq, 'Groundwork'. Another author working within this tradition attempting to reconstruct the paradigm of Islamic governance without projecting Western experience with state, law and politics is Bernard G. Weiss. See e.g. Weiss, *Spirit*.

emphasise that for authors working within this latter tradition, the objective is not always to describe the realities of governance in Muslim communities at a particular point in time and in a particular place, but to describe a paradigm of Islamic governance. When describing this paradigm they use some historical examples as illustrations. For this reason, for example, Hallaq's book was accused of being 'pervaded by nostalgia for the primacy of just, wise and good men, and loving communities, for a dignity and meaningfulness that has been lost; and indeed for a time that never was'.[53] However, my interpretation of this work and of the paradigm that it describes does not claim that there was ever a time to return to which would bring us to a society where this paradigm was realised. Hallaq proceeds by establishing how the functioning of Muslim communities and Islamic law within them is different from modern state framework. He demonstrates that if the modern state emerged and is based on a distinction between fact and value, law and morality, traditional Islamic governance structures did not know this distinction.[54] In doing so he demonstrates how conceptually different the operation of the Islamic governance system was without claiming that it was ever perfectly implemented, without idealising the past.

In terms of scholarly legal developments within Islamic tradition, it is interesting to point out that in compilations of legal knowledge by Muslim scholars, what is called today religious or ritual matters was not separate from strictly legal matters. The portion of these compilations dedicated to religious/ritual matters was quite high. The methodology applied by Muslim scholars to derive rules from available sources on matters related to ritual/religion was exactly the same as that applied to strictly legal matters. However, the dominant Western scholarship excluded these parts of Islamic law from their purview.[55] Thus, from the perspective of Muslim scholarship there was no separation between strictly legal and religious/ritual matters. Another dichotomy characterising modernity that according to Hallaq did not exist in early Islamic tradition is that between law and morality.[56] Hallaq highlights that even the term 'moral' or 'morality' did not exist in classical Arabic language

[53] Lapidus, 'Book Review', 206.

[54] A very interesting discussion around fact/value dichotomy is contained in Doeser and Kraay, *Facts and Values*. This volume contains many contributions from a non-Western perspective, all of which find this dichotomy alien to their own tradition.

[55] See for example Johansen's discussion of Schacht's *Introduction to Islamic Law* criticising its exclusion of worship and ritual: Johansen, *Contingency*, 60.

[56] See Hallaq, *State*, Chapter 4 in general.

because there was no need for a separate term: the legal was imbued with the moral, the moral was the essence of the legal – both were one and the same thing.[57] This happened not because the idea of a moral human being did not exist, but because it was so intimately linked to other aspects of normativity within the society – including what scholars today would identify as strictly legal matters – that there was no need to single out morality as a particular type of normativity.

This Hallaq's assessment of Islamic law is partly supported by early Western scholarship on Islamic law that for a long period of time refused to recognise the quality of 'law' to the Islamic normative system, referring to it as 'deontology'.[58] However, later scholars demonstrated that this description of Islamic law as lacking of technically legal character is erroneous.[59] This in turn led to the already mentioned focus on what was perceived by occidental scholarship as purely legal matters. The specificity of Hallaq's statement relates to the emphasis on the distinctiveness of Islamic normative system as being directed at what Western scholars would describe as morality and law simultaneously and the impossibility of understanding the functions of *fiqh*[60] without taking into account the totality of its parts with their complementary functions.

The capacity of the Islamic normative system to address regulation of community through a different type of channels compared to Western legal and political system is obviously linked to the religious origin of this normative system. However, we will see later that this religious origin is not an impediment to considering how some of the mechanisms used within this normative system could be transposed to other non-religious contexts. Before discussing this possibility we need however to understand more precisely how the ordering of community functioned, what

57 Ibid., 82.

58 See in particular the works of Snouck Hurgronje, for example Bousquet and Schacht, *Selected Works*. See also Goldziher, *Vorlesungen*.

59 See in particular the work of Joseph Schacht, who is credited with making several important contributions to the study of Islamic law in Western academia, including a clear articulation of Islamic law as a legal system, not simply a deontology. See e.g. Schacht, *Introduction*.

60 *Fiqh* (in Arabic meaning 'understanding', 'comprehension') is a general term often used to designate the legal science. Today the more broadly used term *shari'a* (meaning 'way', 'path to water') designates the ideal totality of God's will as revealed to the prophet Muhammad. The widely occurring confusion between these two terms with the predominance of *shari'a* used to designate the totality of law leads to sacralisation of something that is a humanly constructed phenomenon. See more on this distinction and its importance in Abou El Fadl, *Speaking*, 32–35; and Yahyaoui Krivenko, *Women*, 47–48.

specific mechanisms were used to constrain arbitrary use of power and promote the well-being of individual members of the community. Two interrelated essential structures within this normative mechanism need to be highlighted. The first structure relates to what Hallaq names as the moral technologies of the self. The second structure emerges from Hallaq's description of the equivalent to the separation of powers within this Islamic normative and regulatory system.

a) Moral Technologies of the Self

Hallaq starts by explaining that each type of ordering produces certain types of individuals that are best suited for the maintenance and continuing operation of this ordering. For instance, he demonstrates that the state form produces individuals that leave in a separation between 'I' and 'we', between rationality and practical ethics.[61] He contrasts this state subject with the subjectivities produced by Islamic ordering. In order to fully appreciate the specificities of Islamic subjectivities, it is important to read the Islamic normative system, or what is usually called Islamic law as a whole, without separating 'purely' legal matters from ritual or religious matters.[62] Hallaq demonstrates how different aspects of ritual – such as purification, prayer, fasting or almsgiving – prepared the subject of Islamic normative system to the participation in what is regarded from the Western perspective as the strictly legal sphere: 'The morality that activated willing submission to the authority of the "law" was *constituted* by these performative acts [rituals].'[63]

Hallaq emphasises the aspect of care of the self embodied in this approach to ordering and regulating life of the community. This care of the self is mainly achieved through daily repetition of certain acts: through training.[64] As a consequence, morality and ethical conduct become part of what human beings are, not simply some theoretical values existing outside and independently of individuals imposed on them out of a sense of obligation or duty.[65] From this intimate link between performative acts and legal regulation emerges a particular

[61] Hallaq, *State*, 106–108.

[62] Although this distinction is pre-modern, in the mainstream literature on Islamic law the distinction between the former (*mu'āmalāt*) and the latter (*'ibādāt*) is maintained in order to relegate *'ibādāt* to a sphere of non-legal, non-important from the legal point of view and thus distort the understanding of Islamic law and the way in which one shaped and influenced the other, thus creating a coherent normative system. Hallaq, *State*, 115–116 in particular.

[63] Ibid., 118, emphasis in the original. [64] Ibid., 132. [65] Ibid., 135.

type of individuals ready to follow law out of their own will without the need for coercion and enforcement. However, if the individual is ready to comply with the law, those who make the law, who have the influence on the law-making process, possess the power to influence and perhaps misuse people's readiness to comply with law for their own personal benefit. Therefore, the Islamic governance system created a second mechanism that can be called separation of powers.

b) Separation of Powers in Islam

What is called here 'separation of powers' is very different from the traditional Western concept of separation of powers. However, the use of the term is justified to the extent that both mechanisms ensure that the operation of the normative is separated from the political influence as well as from personal preferences. The main purpose of the mechanism discussed in this section is to ensure that those who have influence over rules that will apply to the Muslim community and its individual members do not misuse the power they possess for personal purposes. It also ensures that political leaders are unable to influence the production of the normative. In order to understand this mechanism, it is important first to grasp the functional differentiation of roles related to governance, power, and law as they emerge from the paradigm of Islamic governance. These different roles and the associated functional differentiation were to various degrees part of historical Muslim communities. However, one should be aware of the fact that they never existed in their pure forms. Similarly to Western ideals such as democracy or rule of law, while we can identify instances where these concepts are quite well implemented, it is more difficult to affirm that they were ever fully realised.

The governance structure within this society was based on a functional differentiation that has no parallels in the modern nation-state. The best way of presenting this functional differentiation is by comprehending the different roles played by different individuals that have to deal with the normative regulation of conduct. In this regard, the central role of a jurist-interpreter (*mujtahid*)[66] and its relationship to other roles is of crucial importance. The jurist-interpreter is a specialist who due to his knowledge

[66] There are two Arabic terms that are used to designate the jurist-interpreter: *mujtahid* and *mufti*. As far as their qualifications (technical knowledge they are required to possess) are concerned, they are identical. The difference resides in their broader social role within Islamic society. While *mujtahid* is simply somebody who acquired sufficient qualifications to exercise his own reasoning in deducing rules from primary sources, a *mufti* has a legal obligation to issue opinions on law-related matters to anybody who requests such an

and skills is recognised by the surrounding community as possessing the authority to derive rules suitable for application in concrete cases from indicators contained in primary sources.[67] His position within the normative field of Islamic societies was particularly important owing to his capacity and authority to develop and articulate new normative standards or more precisely new rules for application in concrete situations. Within this context 'new' always maintains the link to the primary sources and principles contained therein. Hallaq describes this authority of jurists-interpreters as epistemic[68] since the basis of authority was knowledge and qualifications obtained by a particular person within certain fields, such as Arabic language, history, knowledge of the Quran and *sunna*, to name just a few.[69] The best way of understanding the role played by the jurist-interpreter is through a comparison to other functions fulfilled within the normative field of Islamic societies by other types of specialists.

opinion. Therefore, in addition to all the qualifications a *mujtahid* possesses, a *mufti* shall also be an upright, pious person who faithfully follows religion and law. See Hallaq, *Origins*, 146–147. However, in other contexts it was suggested that there is no difference between a *mujtahid* and a *mufti*, as it seems that a *mujtahid* as a highly qualified specialist would always be solicited to provide his advice on some issues and thus perform the role of a *mufti*, therefore requiring him to be a pious person. See e.g. a discussion of the role of *mufti* and *mujtahid* in Abdalla, 'Australian Muslims'. A different question is whether a *mufti* (person giving advice on juridical matters) can be a non-*mujtahid*. On this see e.g. Weiss, *Spirit*, 133–134. He affirms that 'A nonmujtahid mufti was, admittedly, something of an anomaly (. . .)' (Ibid., 133). See also Hallaq, 'Ifta'. For the reasons of simplicity this distinction is not taken further in the subsequent discussion, and the term 'jurist-interpreter' is used as a generic term to denote the paradigm of highly qualified specialists who were able to derive new rules from indicators and advise other non-qualified believers on appropriate normative standards in particular situations.

67 The Quran and *sunna* as the two textual sources of Islam contain often only very general statements about the appropriate conduct in certain situations. They almost never provide enough detail to allow for a clear picture of a conduct a believer needs to adopt in similar situations. Many situations are not addressed directly at all. This does not mean that there is no statement in either the Quran or *sunna* that could serve as a basis for a possible development of a concrete rule. However, because of the generality of statements contained in textual sources, the specific methodology for derivation of concrete rules from more general statements was required. This methodology represents the essence of Islamic law (*fiqh*) and was the domain of purview of jurists-interpreter.

68 Hallaq, *Origins*, 66. See also a very similar description of this juristic authority by Abu el Fadl as 'authoritative not because they are in authority – the formal position is irrelevant – but because of the social perception of being authorities on the set of instructions (indicators) that point to God's Way.' Abou el Fadl, *Speaking*, 53, 9–85 in general.

69 There is no agreement among scholars on the required qualifications. While a number of core qualifications can be discerned, their precise contours always remained subject to debate. See e.g. ibid.

The first significant distinction is drawn between the jurist-interpreter and the judge (*qāḍī*). Judges' functions evolved significantly over time. During its crystallisation as a distinct and specialised function, it became focused on 'conflict resolution and legal administration'.[70] At the early stages of development of the Islamic normative system, judges were not required to possess legal knowledge.[71] Their knowledge of the community within which they lived and its functions, including its customs and habits,[72] and their capacity to mediate between disputing parties were far more important.[73] Judges' efforts in resolving disputes between parties were focused more on a fullest-possible understanding of the social relationships between litigating parties and possible future implications of different outcomes than on a strict application of a black-letter law.[74] Thus, the main function of judges was gathering of evidence and hearing of witnesses, which included a major element of investigating integrity and rectitude of all participants.[75]

When a more difficult question of law surfaced within a particular process, the judge would resort to legal opinions (*fatwās*) issued by jurists-interpreters. The existing research attests to the significant role played by jurists-interpreters in assisting judges with correct interpretation and application of points of law ranging from regular presence of jurists-interpreters in the courts of law to routine reference of difficult cases to jurists-interpreters.[76] Obviously, at times it happened that a person assuming function of a judge possessed the required qualifications of a jurist-interpreter. However, significantly, there is a strong tradition of jurists-interpreters refusing and avoiding appointments as judges.[77] This was due to the fact that judges were appointed and paid by the political leader (*calif*), while jurists-interpreters, in order to maintain their position of epistemic authority, dissociated themselves from political influences, including through the maintenance of their financial independence.[78]

[70] Hallaq, *Origins*, 57.

[71] Hallaq provides examples of illiterate *qāḍīs* and also describes the way disputes were settled as being based on common sense and general religious knowledge: Ibid., 34–35; on absence of legal knowledge in general: Ibid., 38.

[72] Hallaq, *Sharīʿa*, 166. [73] See Hallaq, *Origins*, 35, 55; Hallaq, *Sharīʿa*, 36.

[74] See e.g. Rosen, *Anthropology*, 16–19. [75] Hallaq, *Sharīʿa*, 170.

[76] For a general overview see Hallaq, *Sharīʿa*, 177–178. For a more specific analysis of particular parts of Muslim tradition at particular periods see Masud, Brinkley, Powers, 'Muftis', 10–11; Powers, 'Legal Consultation', 93, 94, 96; Mandaville, *Muslim Judiciary*, 71, 11.

[77] Hallaq, *Origins*, 180–181.

[78] Bligh-Abramski, 'Judiciary', 41; and generally Coulson, *Conflicts and Tensions*, 58–76; Hallaq, *Sharīʿa*, 159–196; Abu El Fadl, *Speaking*, 15.

This independence was a guarantee and a sign that their pronouncements on legal issues are based exclusively on their epistemic authority, on their knowledge. This also ensured that jurists-interpreters were free from worldly political influences. Although, in practice the dynamics of the relationship between jurists-interpreters, judges and the ruler were far more complex, authors generally agree on the tendency of jurists-interpreters in maintaining their independence from the political power and rulers being dependent on uncorrupted jurists-interpreters to legitimate their position of power.[79] One last remark on the conduct of hearings before a judge: Very often parties to a dispute would present to a judge opinions of jurists-interpreters of their choice whom they consulted in advance of appearing before the judge.[80] If there was a need to make a choice between opinions of different jurists-interpreters, it would be based on the epistemic reputation of a particular jurist-interpreter that is obviously linked to his skills and knowledge, including the persuasiveness of his argument.[81]

Another role that needs to be distinguished from that of the jurist-interpreter is the role of the author-jurist. This role consisted mainly in the writing of legal manuals and other long treatises on law. Thus, the author-jurist compiled and systematised legal knowledge produced by jurists-interpreters. Again, nothing prevented some jurists-interpreters from writing these compilations. However, fundamentally two activities were performed by two different sets of specialists. While an author-jurist needed training in law similar to that of the jurist-interpreter, the degree of perfection and depth of this knowledge was less demanding than that of the jurist-interpreter.[82]

So what was this particular field of activity exclusively reserved to the jurist-interpreter as the best-qualified specialist? The textual sources of Islam (the Quran and *sunna*) contain a number of pronouncements about the appropriate conduct in different types of situations. These pronouncements are supposed to guide the behaviour of believers at all times and in all places. However, the variety of conditions under which these situations arise and the situations themselves are, in practice, broader than what the primary sources contain, hence, the need for all believers to be able to find guidance for their behaviour even in situations and under conditions that are not directly, clearly and unambiguously addressed in the primary

[79] See e.g. Bligh-Abramski, 'Judiciary'; Hallaq, 'Juristic Authority', 243–258; Hallaq, *State*, 37–73; Abu El Fadl, *Islam*, 12–16; Weiss, *Spirit*, 113–144; 172–185.

[80] Masud, Brinkley, Powers, 'Muftis', 9, 11. [81] Ibid. [82] Hallaq, *Sharī'a*, 176–183.

textual sources. Juristic interpretative methodology served this specific need of believers. The methodology developed over time and became a very complex matter requiring a number of skills and vast amount of knowledge. Jurists-interpreters were those specialists who possessed these skills and knowledge and to whom other believers turned when they needed guidance and advice with regard to their behaviour.

One fundamental question that arises with regard to the role of jurists-interpreters is the following: How could a non-specialist possibly know and check that the jurist-interpreter followed the prescribed methodology faithfully? How could a non-specialist ascertain that the specialist's advice was not simply an arbitrary ruling based on his own personal preferences? The seriousness of these questions and the need to find appropriate answers to them becomes more obvious if we remember that, using the same methodology, jurists-interpreters can arrive at different, even opposing results, but also that there are some differences in how the methodology is applied across different groups of specialists (schools of law). According to the fundamental principle of Islamic normative universe, every specialist is deemed correct in his answers (every *mujtahid* is correct).[83] Thus in order to preserve links to the divine as expressed in the primary sources and ensure that advice is guided only by the search for the most faithful solution/answer and not by personal preferences of the specialists, mechanisms of control were required.

The first element of this mechanism was the recognition of the inherent pluralism of Islamic normativity or Islamic law. The diversity of opinions and divergences between scholars were recognised as a blessing and as a richness within Islamic tradition. In order to foster and maintain this diversity, the principle 'every *mujtahid* is correct' emerged very early in the development of Islamic normativity. The principle highlighted the recognition of the fundamental fallibility of human intellect while at the same time recognising the value of intellectual efforts of jurists-interpreters. The pluralism combined with the principle 'every *mujtahid* is correct' also ensured that no group of persons could legitimately claim that only one interpretation or vision of law is valid and thus usurp the power within a particular Islamic society.

The next important element was related to the possibility for believers to select among specialists, combined with the absence of an official system for determination of those qualified as jurists-interpreters. Since knowing God's expectations regarding each individual's behaviour (law)

[83] Abou El Fadl, *Speaking*, 32–33.

and acting accordingly is conceived in Islam as a fundamental religious duty of every believer, every Muslim is expected to understand and actively engage with the normative. Becoming a jurist-interpreter was potentially open to any believer and achievable without financial sacrifice.[84] For those believers who were not qualified as jurists-interpreters, this meant a duty to diligently select a jurist-interpreter whom they wished to follow.[85] Diligence in this regard signified gaining as much as possible understanding of this particular jurist-interpreter's approach to legal reasoning as well as acquire knowledge of his piety, moral standing and similar personal qualities. This was quite easily achievable task because jurists-interpreters did not form an elite class, but permeated all classes and social strata of society.[86] On the other hand, the standing of jurists-interpreters, including the precise enumeration of qualifications they needed to acquire has never been officialised or sanctioned by the ruling authorities.[87] Therefore, the decision about who is qualified as a jurist-interpreter and who is the best jurist-interpreter was left to ordinary believers who would, through their choices and through their solicitation of opinions of jurists-interpreters, determine the standing of a particular specialist as a recognised and renowned jurist-interpreter.

The third element within the system was related to financial aspects of jurist-interpreters activities. These financial aspects are of a twofold nature: they encompass the accessibility of services and financial independence of jurists-interpreters. Accessibility of advice and services provided by jurists-interpreters was one of the fundamental pillars of the Islamic governance system. In order for the ordinary believer to be able to access freely the specialised knowledge of jurists-interpreters and choose without constraints those whom he/she deems most qualified and pious, the free nature of services was essential. This element also allowed keeping the mechanism related to the free choice of specialists by individual believers running efficiently. The second financial aspect relates to jurist-interpreters' financial independence. The provision of free services to believers meant that jurists-interpreters had to find other sources of income. Simultaneously, as mentioned above, jurists-interpreters needed to maintain their independence from the ruling elite. Therefore, they could not rely on a systematic payment from the ruler. This led to the

84 On the legal education and easiness with which any believer could take part in it, see e.g. Hallaq, *Sharī'a*, 125–158.

85 Weiss, *Spirit*, 128–129; Abou El Fadl, *Speaking*, 51.

86 See e.g. Lapidus, *Muslim Cities*, 108.

87 Hallaq, *Sharī'a*, 125–158; Weiss, *Spirit*, 128–129.

creation of other mechanisms ensuring sources of income for jurists-interpreters. Many of them had other professions or qualifications that constituted their main source of income. Occasionally, they would accept positions and services remunerated by the ruler. However, this would be done in such a way as not to overshadow their independence.[88]

As a result, a particular dynamic emerges whereby specialists who have influence on the content of the normative, exercise their norm-setting competence within a framework that creates external conditions and internal incentives most favourable to an independent and purely epistemologically oriented activity. This in turn results in the effective pre-emption of the arbitrary use of power by jurists-interpreters themselves but also by rulers or political power-holders. Of course, rulers or political power-holders could always attempt to manipulate opinions of jurists-interpreters by brute force. There are many examples of physical repression of jurists-interpreters through the centuries of Islamic history. The political power-holders could also simply disregard the opinion of jurists-interpreters and act as they wish. However, in both cases the ruler or political power holder loses his legitimacy as a political leader of Muslim community. Therefore, in the history of Islamic societies the rulers had never acted as if they were indifferent to the opinion of jurist-interpreters. They adopted various strategies aimed at justifying their actions from within the juristic discourse by attempting to exercise some degree of control over the discourse of jurists-interpreters. For instance, they would privilege a particular school or stream, labelling others as apostates or blasphemers,[89] or attempt to develop strategies at influencing at least some portions of jurists-interpreters through financial means.[90] However, paradigmatically, this structure represents a particular assemblage that ensured norm-production guided by shared normative values of a community. Within this norm-production different mechanisms were built in that operated as guardians of continuing pluralism and

[88] On the complexities of the relationship between the rulers and jurists-interpreters, see e.g. Zaman, 'Caliphs', 1–36. However, despite all the complexities of the relationship between jurists-interpreters and caliphs that involved collaboration, the author concludes that 'caliph does not define the law' (Ibid., 36), which confirms the vision of Islamic governance paradigm presented here.

[89] A symbolic historical example is the period known as *mihna* and events that preceded and followed it when there was an attempt by the ruling dynasty to strategically utilise and impose a particular stream of thought. See e.g. Patton, *Hanbal*, or Wielke, *Mihna*.

[90] A particularly telling case represents the way political power slowly found ways of influencing the legal profession through the use of the institution of *waqf* (charitable foundation). See on this e.g. Hallaq, *Sharīʿa*, 142–158.

re-negotiation of values thus allowing for a full participation of all believers in the elaboration of normative standards of the community. This in turn ensured respect and dignity of every believer – very much in line with human rights and constitutionalist ideals – who thus fully belonged to the norm-producing assemblage.

We can summarise the essential elements of this structure as follows: (1) celebrated and actively promoted pluralism with a clear absence of hierarchy; (2) free access to jurists-interpreters (norm producers) that itself included such sub-elements as (a) promotion of diligence (understood as selection based on relevant criteria such as knowledge and piety) on the part of general public in selecting their preferred norm-producer, (b) possibility for general public to get knowledge about the qualifications and attitude of norm-producers personally even if indirectly, (c) absence of sanctioning authority of power-holders with regard to the recognition of qualifications of norm-producers. Finally, the third element (3) consisted of the financial independence of jurists-interpreters that signified independence from both the power-holder (jurists-interpreters could not be paid regularly by power-holders for their services or could never be considered as somehow employed by the ruling elite) and general public (in the sense that the provision of services by jurists-interpreters was for free; while this helped maintain the genuine character of the second element, it also ensured that a wealthy member of general public could not manipulate the opinion provided by the jurist-interpreter through a higher payment).

We should remember that this structure compared by Hallaq to the separation of powers was intimately linked to the moral technologies of the self that were discussed in the previous section. These moral technologies of the self acted as an additional safeguard against possible misuses of certain elements mentioned above. For instance, it helped ensure that selection of jurists-interpreters by the general public would be based on genuine diligence and not simply strategic personal preferences for those jurists-interpreters whose opinion would be most beneficial to a member of the general public in a particular case.

This structure seems very intriguing and different from anything the modern Western world has experienced. However, the question of the suitability of this structure or any of its components for the contemporary global governance context emerges, especially in light of the opposition between the religious foundation of the Islamic tradition and the postulated secular character of the contemporary international legal system. Can there at all be any lessons to learn for a secular system from a system that is based on religion?

2 *Islamic Tradition and Lessons for Contemporary Global Governance*

From the outset, it is important to relativise both the religious character of the Islamic governance and the secular character of the international legal system. Islamic governance and its normative field are based on the Quran and a set of beliefs inherent in Islam. However, as will be demonstrated below, the mechanisms used within the Islamic normative and governance structures can function without their religious fundament. On the other hand, we have to remind ourselves constantly that the contemporary international legal system, although secular in theory, emerged historically from a profoundly Christian and European experience. Thus, its structures and mechanisms are profoundly religious in the sense that they were shaped by the particular religious experience of Europe, even if constituting itself at times in opposition to this experience. Thus, if we envisage here whether any useful lessons can be learned by public international law from the Islamic experience, we have to focus on the compatibility or transferability of mechanisms and structures from one tradition to another. Thus, in line with Deleuze and Guattari's method the fundamental question will be about 'how it functions'. Based on the understanding of the modalities of functioning of both mechanisms, we can then provide a better answer to the question of compatibility or transferability of mechanisms and its parts.

Within the Islamic tradition the jurist-interpreter occupies a central place. However, his precise role within the mechanism is very complex. He is both one of the building blocks of the system, but also an important connector between the powerful ruling elite and the everyday life of human beings. He also connects the political and the normative while at the same time ensuring a separation between the two. One could imagine the position of the jurist-interpreter as a piece through which the political flows and becomes transformed into the normative before being injected into the everyday life of people. If it is not possible to transform the political into the normative, it becomes rejected. The same flow can operate into another direction: everyday life and demands of people are transformed into the normative to the extent possible and then flow into and influence the political and thus the rulers. Therefore, it is important to understand what allows this transformation into the normative. What is the central mechanism within this piece that performs the selective and the transformative function?

This particular mechanism includes a series of extra-normative dynamics that ensure that pronouncements of jurists-interpreters on normative questions are as much as possible based on purely cognitive/epistemological foundations without any influence by such considerations as financial, political, personal/private relationships and similar unrelated factors. Thus, the system ensured that the jurist-interpreter has all required knowledge in order to engage in the rule-producing process, but in addition it also introduced a series of conditions allowing the jurist-interpreter to live and engage in the rule-producing process without being manipulated through his human needs and necessities. However, taking into account that some people do not content themselves with just basic necessities and might desire more wealth or power and thus be tempted to corrupt the epistemological purity of the normative production process in order to satisfy these desires, an additional element was integrated into this control mechanism. This element can be called 'moral' in reference to the personal integrity and conduct of jurists-interpreters in everyday life. This element functioned through embeddedness of jurists-interpreters in their surrounding community. Living side by side with people who come for advice and guidance, whose life generates needs for rules that jurist-interpreters formulate also meant that daily behaviour and attitude of jurists-interpreters could be scrutinised by the surrounding community. If ordinary people suspected that a particular jurist-interpreter was not sincerely devoted to the search for truth, that he did not follow his own pronouncements, they would easily turn away from him to another jurist-interpreter with more integrity and higher moral standards. This simultaneous acceptance of diversity within a given range of methodological approaches and possibility for the followers to select and follow the approach of their choice functioned as a controlling mechanism.

We can see from this brief depiction of the mechanism that a specific religious belief is not central to its functioning. However, something similar to morality in the form of piety of persons engaged in the epistemic activity is central to the successful functioning of the mechanism. As highlighted previously, law and morality cannot be regarded as separate categories within this traditional Islamic paradigm. However, in the absence of a better term we will refer to this piety element as morality, keeping in mind that it constitutes part and parcel of the normative paradigm that is discussed and that is indistinguishable from law as described above.

Morality is not alien to human rights and the functioning of international system. Most importantly, morality is enshrined in requirements set for people who occupy important decision-making positions within international system, especially judges and decision-makers in quasi-judicial organs. Thus, for instance, judges of the International Court of Justice (ICJ) are expected to be 'persons of high moral character, who possess the qualifications required in their respective countries for appointment to the highest judicial offices, or are juris-consults of recognized competence in international law'.[91] Similar provisions can be found in relation to any judicial or quasi-judicial function or other positions of responsibility within international institutions and structures.[92] It is significant that the moral character of a person is explicitly stated as a requirement on pair with high level of knowledge in the

[91] Art. 2 Statute of the ICJ.

[92] See e.g. members of the Human Rights Committee 'shall be persons of high moral character and recognized competence in the field of human rights' (International Covenant on Civil and Political Rights, 16 December 1966, 999 UNTS 171, 28(2)); provisions for other human rights treaty monitoring bodies indicate the following requirements: 'experts of high moral standing and acknowledged impartiality' (Convention on the Elimination of All Forms of Racial Discrimination, 7 March 1966, 660 UNTS 195, Art. 8(1)); 'experts of high moral standing and recognized competence in the field of human rights' (Convention Against Torture and Other Cruel, Inhumane or Degrading Treatment or Punishment, 10 December 1984, 1465 UNTS 85, Art. 17(1)); 'high moral standing and competence in the field covered by the Convention' (Convention on the Elimination of All Forms of Discrimination Against Women, 18 December 1979, 1249 UNTS 13 Art. 17); 'high moral standing and recognized competence in the field covered by this Convention' (Convention on the Rights of the Child, 20 November 1989, 1577 UNTS 3, Art. 43(2)); 'high moral standing, impartiality and recognized competence in the field covered by the Convention' (International Convention on the Protection of Rights of All Migrant Workers and Members of Their Families, 18 December 1990, 2220 UNTS 3, Art. 72 (1)b)); 'high moral standing and recognized competence and experience in the field covered by the present Convention' (Convention on the Rights of Persons with Disabilities, 13 December 2006, 2515 UNTS 3, Art. 34(3)); 'high moral character and recognized competence in the field of human rights' (International Convention for the Protection of All Persons from Enforced Disappearances, 20 December 2006, 2716 UNTS 3, Art. 26(1)); with regard to the mandate-holders within special procures of the Human Rights Council, 'The following general criteria will be of paramount importance while nominating, selecting and appointing mandate-holders: (a) expertise; (b) experience in the field of the mandate; (c) independence; (d) impartiality; (e) personal integrity; and (f) objectivity' Art. 39 of the A/HRC/RES/5/1 18.6.2007; beyond the broad area of human rights the requirement also applies. For a few examples see Art. 2(1) of the Statute of the International Tribunal for the Law of the Sea requiring judges to be 'persons enjoying the highest reputation for fairness and integrity and of recognized competence in the field of the law of the sea.' (Annex to the Convention on the Law of the Sea, 10 December 1982, 1833 UNTS, 3) and Art. 36(3) a) of the Rome Statute of the International Criminal Court, 17 July 1998, 2187 UNTS 3 stipulating that judges be 'chosen from among persons of high moral character, impartiality and integrity who possess the qualifications required in their respective States for appointment to the highest judicial offices'.

relevant area. However, the practice of selecting persons to these decision-making positions pays only a very marginal attention to the requirement of high moral standing. In practice, no efficient mechanism for probing the moral character has been developed, except the obvious absence of any information to the contrary.[93] Also, taking into account a very distant relationship between candidates and institutions to which they are appointed very often those who select candidates have to rely on the affirmation of those who nominate the candidates that the requirement of high moral character is fulfilled. For example, writing on the requirement of high moral character of the judges of the ICJ, Taslim Olawale Elias who served himself as a judge and a president of the ICJ describes the requirement of high moral character as 'more or less the equivalent of unimpeachable conduct as a public figure; in other words, the candidate need not be an angel, though he must not be only little better than a rascal'.[94] He adds: 'The test may be a subjective one insofar as his state of origin is concerned, but the candidate's character is to be judged objectively by the international community – which may have to rely on the nominating national groups.'[95]

Thus, contrary to the mechanism of Islamic governance that included concrete safeguards allowing a constant evaluation and re-evaluation of the piety and faithfulness to the required moral, cognitive and epistemological standards of persons who had the power to influence outcomes of concrete cases, in international law the requirement of high moral character operates rather as a presumption that stands true until evidence to the contrary emerges. Also the distance, both physical and symbolic, that separates decision-makers of various international bodies from those whose lives these decisions affect makes impossible a connection comparable to the dynamic present in the Islamic paradigm of governance between the believer and the jurist-interpreter. Therefore, in order for this mechanism to become embedded into the practice of international law it will be necessary to rethink selection and nomination processes in a way that ensures efficient check of both cognitive or epistemological and

[93] Another notion existent in international law that might appear to come close to the requirement of piety in the Islamic paradigm is that of judicial independence and impartiality. The parallel however is misguided because in the judicial practice at both national and international levels independence and impartiality are only evaluated at the public appearance level. They do not go so far as to scrutinise the everyday attitudes and behaviour of decision-makers. Also, independence and impartiality is only one aspect of what the requirement of piety implies in the Islamic governance paradigm discussed here.

[94] Elias, *New Horizons*, 73. [95] Ibid., 73–74.

the moral elements by all potentially affected persons. Moreover this mechanism should be actionable not only once, at the moment of nomination or selection, but continuously. If international decision-making bodies are democratised in line with the paradigm of Islamic governance, this would make less problematic the rise in pre-eminence of courts and tribunals as arenas of legitimation and practice of constituent power as indicated by Thornhill.[96] This will potentially help to achieve a required shift in mechanisms able to overcome the exclusion/inclusion dynamic that is discussed in the final chapter.

C Conclusions

The examination of processes and mechanisms used in the ancient Greek and early Islamic societies to control power and prevent its abuse provide two complementary insights that can inform the future of global constitutionalism and its uneasy relationship to human rights. The ancient Greece and its experience with the transition to written law understood as available to human beings for use but also misuse, made the society more egalitarian and more focused on the autonomous individual within the juridico-political sphere. However, this process happened at the expense of the previously predominant case- and context-specific search for justice that ensured broader balance and peace within community but also that each individual comes out of each dispute or conflict with a sense of having achieved a best possible outcome in any given circumstances. The problematic aspect of this latter mechanism within the ancient Greek context related to its elitist character that excluded broad layers of population from decision-making. The turn to written law underpinned by the idea of political equality helped to correct the elitist character of the mechanism to some extent but this also to a significant degree destroyed the mechanism itself. Therefore, the paradigm of early Islamic governance is used as an alternative way of correcting the elitism without losing the focus of the mechanism on community, context- and case-specific solutions.

Although one of the elements of the historical experience of early Islamic societies with the ordering is obviously religious, the previous section demonstrated that the paradigm of Islamic governance that forms the basis for discussion can function also in other non-religious contexts. We have seen that this paradigm or mechanism consists of two

[96] See Chapter 2, section 'Thornhill and the Fusion of Law and Politics'.

structures: moral technologies of the self and separation of powers. Within the structure of separation of powers the elements of pluralism and absence of hierarchy together with the free selection of norm-producers by all potentially affected as well as their financial independence are present. Within the element of free selection of norm-producers diligence in the selection process, personal (although not necessarily direct) knowledge of the norm-producers and absence of the sanctioning power of the state were highlighted. When envisioning the application of this paradigm to the contemporary realities of the global order several of these elements appear challenging. In particular, avoiding the sanctioning power of the state or institutions embedded in state structures as far as qualifications of decision-makers are concerned appears impossible today. However, this sanctioning power of the state is to some degree relativised at the international level because of the plurality of states and thus sites of sanctioning. Nevertheless, we should not forget the need for caution with regard to state thinking highlighted by Bourdieu. The realisation of other elements at the global level while very difficult is not completely impossible to envisage. This would obviously require significant reforms and restructuring. Some of the ways forward integrating insights gained from this chapter will be formulated in the final section.

At the point of encounter between the ancient Greek and the Islamic traditions the significance of community is reaffirmed echoing the preoccupations discussed within the paradigm of the political. Despite this refocus on community, the individual human being does not disappear but re-emerges in a new light as active through the very living shaping the content of the normative. The concept of human rights in its traditional Western understanding has no place anymore but the care for the well-being of both community and each of its individual members remains central and ensured by a different type of mechanism than one embedded in the concept of human rights. This mechanism is not based on exclusion/inclusion dynamic but makes possible to translate normativity into an everyday practice that imbues life of every single person and simultaneously creates a sense of belonging.

4

From Inclusion to Belonging

The contemporary thought on global constitutionalism conceals within its heart a fundamental contradiction between its purpose and the mechanisms it uses to achieve this purpose. Within Western constitutional tradition the goal of constitutionalism was broadly defined as the protection of individuals against arbitrary use of power. However, the mechanisms that have been revealed through the analysis of paradigms that shape global constitutionalism today are all based on an exclusion/inclusion dynamic that necessarily produces arbitrary and unjust results for some individuals. Thus, the individual is positioned as the centre of preoccupations of global constitutionalism with rights protections that guarantee freedom, autonomy and equality to every human being. The inclusion into the benefit of rights is always and necessarily only partial. First, as described in Chapter 1, the traditional concept of citizenship that still determines whether and to what extent individuals can claim rights is based on the inclusion of some and exclusion of others from its benefit. Second, and more problematically, the very functioning of human rights as a mechanism of inclusion necessarily presupposes exclusion as its reverse side. However broad the circle of inclusion, as long as the mechanism itself is based on inclusion, exclusion will always accompany it. Similar considerations apply to the paradigm of the state, which, as a monopolising and universalising device, necessarily excludes opinions, ways of life and practices that contradict its own discourse and thus harms and excludes certain categories of people. Neither traditional constitutional rights, nor international human rights provide a remedy in this regard. Although theoretically both are aimed at protecting individuals against the state, the examination of their functioning reveals that in practice they protect all social subsystems and most importantly the state as the form that the political system takes. Therefore, human rights, as a central building block of global constitutionalism, are also the main mechanism that maintains the exclusion/inclusion dynamic within all paradigms that are part of global constitutionalism. As long as the discourse of human rights and the ensuing exclusion/inclusion dynamic are part of the global constitutionalism, the global constitutionalism will never be able to achieve its aim and will always be vulnerable to various criticisms because of the above-mentioned contradiction between its aims and the mechanisms it uses.

In order for global constitutionalism to overcome the contradiction that hinders its unfolding, a shift away from exclusion/inclusion to a different type of mechanism that is better attuned to global constitutionalism's aim is needed. The nature of this mechanism and its functioning emerge from the suggestions towards paradigm shifts in Chapter 1 and examination of alternative mechanisms of power control in Chapter 3. This mechanism that is proposed here is based on the notion of belonging inspired by writings of Agamben. In Agamben's philosophy, belonging has a particular meaning. Most importantly, as emphasised in the discussion of his alternative vision of the political, belonging is not determined by any condition or characteristic that would unite a particular group of human beings, nor by absence of any condition, but by the belonging itself. Even the humanity of human beings or their dignity cannot be postulated as underlying the notion of belonging. Belonging is being in common of whatever singularities. Agamben also uses the notion of contact, as opposed to relation, which sheds more light on belonging, as articulated here. While relation is constitutive and representative, contact is unrepresentable 'because it consists precisely in a representative void, that is, in the deactivation and inoperativity of every representation'.[1] In this sense belonging can bring about the deactivation or destitution of the two opposites that activate the exclusion/inclusion mechanism of global constitutionalism as it operates today.

What would this mean concretely for the global ordering? How can this belonging function within contemporary practices? First, it should be cautioned that from the perspective of systems theory, which served as a basis for revealing the mechanism underlying the human rights functioning, as well as from the perspective of Agamben's theorisation of coming community that underlies the idea of belonging, the way forward cannot consist of proposing a plan or formulating conclusions.[2] However, both of them recognise the need and usefulness of new theoretical developments.

[1] Agamben, *Use*, 237.

[2] For Luhmann, because social systems are autopoietic and change their own structures only through evolution, society cannot be planned (see e.g. Luhmann, 'World Society'). For Agamben, 'we must decisively call into question the commonplace according to which is it

For Luhamnn, at the very least, a theory can 'change the ways in which the societal system can use theories as instruments of self-observation'.[3] Agamben also acknowledges the need to 'think different strategies'[4] and even 'imagine . . . translating into act the action of a destituent potential in a constituted political system'.[5] Therefore, what follows is not meant to be a conclusion, a final word on the matter, but should be read as suggestions and thoughts on these different strategies.

In the contemporary international law literature, global constitutionalism remains one of the very few fields where idealistic aspirations stay alive. Sharing this idealistic aspiration, the idea of happy life in common on the global scale, the present study does not argue for its demise or displacement of the terminology. The term constitutionalism, in keeping its idealistic core, can reorient itself towards different mechanisms and acquire new functions and meanings, just like the term *nómos*, which changed radically in meaning from 'custom' or 'arrangement' to 'written law', preserving the core idea of an order accepted by those who live under it. This study provided a critical overview of several core paradigms defining the current state of global constitutionalism as well as of its central mechanism: human rights. The critical overview of mechanisms, their functioning and some suggestions formulated along the way prepared the ground for the formulation of the overall strategy that could free the project of global constitutionalism from its contradictions, namely a move away from the mechanism of exclusion/inclusion to that of belonging. This move from inclusion to belonging is radical in several ways and cannot be a simple matter of new institutional practices nor of the establishment of new institutions. What is required is a change in practices, a shift in ways of being that affect the global and the international. This shift is intimately tied to the continuous effort of rethinking familiar notions and concepts. Three of these notions were identified in the first chapter of this study: the individual, the state and the political. Some ways of overcoming conventional thinking on individual, state and politics were presented. These conceptual efforts are crucial and indispensable. However, they need to be accompanied by a practice, a 'translation into act' in constituted global political system we have today. Therefore, the paradigm shifts were formulated in Chapter 1 with the existing practices and conditions of their unfolding in mind.

a good rule that an enquiry commence with a *pars destruens* and conclude with a *pars construens*.' (Agamben, *Use*, xiii).

[3] Luhmann, 'World Society', 137. [4] Agamben, *Use*, 266.

[5] Ibid., 278. Agamben openly acknowledges that this task is beyond the scope of his study.

In relation to the individual, it was suggested that there is a need for individuals to become active and relevant at the level of international law immediately, without mediation by states in order for the global to become the space for an active confrontation of modalities of exclusion. Confronting the modalities of exclusion openly without hiding behind a claim for inclusion could constitute a first step towards the act of depositing the very dynamic of exclusion/inclusion. Also, because the focus is not on the exclusion as such, but on its modalities, the relational logic of exclusion/inclusion could also be deactivated. The example of a private sponsorship of refugees programme provided a practical model for such a practice, highlighting the need to overcome mediation by states and state centricity in such practices.

More specifically, in relation to the state, the need to identify and question the constant presence of the state form and state thinking as a structuring device was highlighted. While both the state form and state thinking are problematic from the perspective of global constitutionalism's goal because they act as monopolising and universalising devices that exclude all incompatible ideas, knowledge and practices, state thinking is more pervasive and less visible, making its uncovering more difficult. As examples of work of Teubner and Krisch have demonstrated, even when some authors attempt to overcome the state form, they usually do so without noticing the continuing operation of state thinking.

The state form is closely linked to the currently predominant vision of the political that, being based on exclusion/inclusion dynamic, uses state's monopolising and universalising power to stabilise the bounded community within each particular unit. Most disturbingly, this vision of the political is linked to the friend/enemy distinction so clearly articulated by Schmitt, which implies the real possibility of fight and physical killing. While Schmitt contended that this is the only possible view of the political, this study opened up a different view of the political that redefines community as inessential belonging, being in contact without a relationship.

These strategies for overcoming the dominant paradigms of global constitutionalism indicate a way forward for global constitutionalism as a practice of depositing and rending inoperative the existing dichotomies, most importantly the exclusion/inclusion dynamic. This presupposes the overcoming of state form in order for the underlying structure of exclusion/inclusion to become irrelevant. In the process of overcoming the state form human beings, humanity as inessential belonging of whatever singularities emerges as a multitude in motion. In this regard it is important to highlight that the future of constitutionalism is necessarily global or world-related.

Constitutionalism that is true to its purpose of happy life in common cannot be international or state-centred. The traditional literature on global constitutionalism postulates human rights as that central mechanism that allows individuals to become the heart of concern, active actors and participants. However, the analysis performed in Chapter 2 has clearly demonstrated that far from focusing on individuals, human rights support and maintain the exclusion/inclusion dynamic that is so essential to the state form. Human rights in their essence represent a mechanism allowing the state to achieve stability and continue to function efficiently. Therefore, similarly to the state form, human rights are antithetical to the idea of global constitutionalism. Therefore, the question arises as to what mechanisms could allow global constitutionalism to work towards its aim? What is needed for global constitutionalism to overcome its dependence on state form and human rights?

The answer to this question is not easy to find, and as both Agamben and Luhmann indicate, there can be no definitive project, no final conclusion. However this does not mean that no theories or alternative conceptualisations can be proposed, no alternative suggestions formulated. Since the state form and law in the form of human rights have to be overcome, alternatives need to be sought in contexts and experiences that precede both the state and the law. For this reason Chapter 3 examined the experience of ancient Greece with ordering before the emergence of the concept of law in a modern sense and of traditional Islamic society before the state form overtook it. This examination revealed that ordering oriented towards the well-being of the community and each and every member of the community can be conceived without the recourse to law in the modern sense and without the state form.

Within the experience of ancient Greece, the concept of *dike* reveals the possibility of an ordering oriented towards the well-being of the community and all its members without recourse to the notion of law or rights. This ordering is based on a case-by-case context-specific resolution of arising problems and disputes aimed at re-establishing peace and well-being within community without positioning any value or norm as absolute truth. The history of ancient Greece during the period when *dike* was the dominant concept addressing the ordering within the community attests to the success of this mechanism. The demise of this mechanism is linked to the way the relationship between those who decide and those who are subject to decisions was framed. This relationship was characterised by an elitist position of those who decide. Therefore, the success of the mechanism largely depended upon the personal qualities of those who were able to accede to these decision-making positions without providing for a solid check of those personal qualities. This elitism of *dike* as it functioned within ancient Greece led to the emergence of *nómos* in a sense of positive law at the disposal of members of the community as a corrective device. While *nómos* was able to correct the elitism, it ultimately led to the destruction of the mechanism embodied in *dike* and led to the emergence of the modern notions, leading to dominance of the exclusion/inclusion mechanism. Therefore, it was necessary to find a way of freeing the mechanism of *dike* from its elitism while keeping its essence as an ordering oriented towards a case-by-case context-specific resolution of problems and disputes promoting peace and well-being of the community and all its members. The early Islamic governance paradigm offered the required insights in this regard.

The paradigm of Islamic governance is not only non-elitist but also truly participatory: all members of the community are constantly engaged in the negotiation and renegotiation of its normative standards. More significantly, what could be called 'law', or more specifically the normative, is not simply a system that individuals enter and exists when they need it or when they cannot escape it; it is a way of life, an integral element of being. Additionally, it also avoids the distinction between fact and value, between cognitive and normative patterns of responses to problems. In this way something like a cognitive normativity emerges. This is a peculiar pattern that builds a normative tissue through a constant learning from arising cases, their circumstances and peculiarities. The normative element is visible only in the overall orientation of the mechanism towards the well-being of the community and its members (in the Islamic context it is linked to compliance with God's will, but substantively the orientation remains the same). The actual responses to the cases emerge from a learning process where all affected individuals participate. Thus, the ancient Greek and the early Islamic tradition combined allow for thinking different strategies for overcoming the exclusion/inclusion dynamic while maintaining the orientation of global constitutionalism towards the well-being of community and all its members. These strategies also allow for the adaptation of the global ordering to the requirements of global society by imagining a community and politics beyond the exclusion/inclusion dynamic but also to be more responsive to dominant cognitive patterns of the global.

In order for these strategies to be set in motion, it is important to encourage and create conditions favourable to individuals' active and immediate relevance at the global level. Equally important is to reorient the problem-solving function of international law from positivation of law in the form of drafting more and more treaties, codifying more and more rules to case-by-case context-specific solutions. International law needs to develop as a mechanism of response to arising disagreements and problems that pays attention to the details of each individual case and is sensitive to the impact of various possible outcomes on the well-being of community as well as on lives of all potentially affected individuals. Finally, in line with the early Islamic governance paradigm, the model of selecting decision-makers needs to be entirely rethought. The Islamic governance paradigm reveals that the most efficient control over possible abuses of power comes from the constant and active involvement of those who can potentially be affected by decisions in the process of selecting and controlling the qualifications of those who will decide. Thus, direct participation of individuals in the choice of decision-makers is crucial. However, this participation should overcome the institutional framework to be able to become a constant check based on an immediate knowledge of both the cognitive and moral qualifications of decision-makers. It is obvious that in this scenario, the involvement of states and international institutions should with time become obsolete. With the contemporary developments in technology, growing speed and accessibility of information exchange, globalisation creates conditions more favourable to putting these suggestions into action. However, as already mentioned, these strategies need to be constantly accompanied by the continuing intellectual work of rethinking familiar notions and concepts even as we attempt to transform them.

Looking at the global ordering from the constitutionalist perspective forces us to ask the right questions about broader political, societal and communitarian aspects of this ordering's future. However, constitutionalism itself in a traditional sense is not sufficient to provide answers to these questions. This study has also demonstrated that relying on human rights is not sufficient and is even self-defeating. At the very least, theorisation of global constitutionalism should become a space for critical reflections on the fate of human rights and other Western constitutional concepts, especially the reimagination of the global ordering with the ideal of happy life in mind.

BIBLIOGRAPHY

Abdalla, Mohamad, 'Do Australian Muslims Need a Mufti? Analysing the Institution of Ifta in the Australian Context' in Nadirsyah Hosen and Richard Mohr (eds) *Law and Religion in Public Life: A Contemporary Debate* (London and New York: Routledge, 2011) 214–228.

Abou El Fadl, Khaled, *Islam and the Challenge of Democracy*. A 'Boston Review' Book (Princeton: Princeton University Press, 2004).

Abou El Fadl, Khaled, *Speaking in God's Name: Islamic Law, Authority and Women* (Oxford: Oneworld, 2001).

Agamben, Giorgio, 'Bartleby, or on Contingency' in Giorgio Agamben, *Potentialities. Collected Essays in Philosophy*, (Stanford: Stanford University Press, 1999). 243–274.

Agamben, Giorgio, 'Beyond Human Rights' (2008) 15 *Social Engineering* 90–95.

Agamben, Giorgio, *The Coming Community* (Minneapolis: University of Minnesota Press, 1993).

Agamben, Giorgio, *The Highest Poverty: Monastic Rules and the Form-of-Life* (Stanford: Stanford University Press, 2013).

Agamben, Giorgio, *Homo Sacer: Sovereign Power and Bare Life* (Stanford: Stanford University Press, 1998).

Agamben, Giorgio, *Means without End. Notes on Politics* (Minneapolis and London: University of Minnesota Press, 2000).

Agamben, Giorgio, *The Signature of All Things: On Method* (New York: Zone Books, 2009).

Agamben, Giorgio, *The State of Exception* (Chicago: University of Chicago Press, 2005).

Agamben, Giorgio *The Use of Bodies* (Stanford: Stanford University Press, 2016).

An-Na'im, Abdullahi A., 'The Spirit of the Ghost of Islamic Law' (1999) 2 *The Green Bag*, 2D Series 441–447.

Araujo, Father Robert, 'Sovereignty, Human Rights, and Self-Determination: The Meaning of International Law' (2000) 24 *Fordham International Law Journal* 1477–1532.

Arendt, Hannah, *The Origins of Totalitarianism* (Cleveland and New York: Meridian Books. The World Publishing Company, 1958).

Balibar, Etienne, *Nous, citoyens d'Europe? Les frontières, l'Etat, le peuple* (Paris: Editions de la découverte, 2001). Translated into English as *We the People of Europe? Reflections on Transnational Citizenship* (Princeton: Princeton University Press, 2004).

Bellamy, Richard, *Political Constitutionalism: A Republican Defence of the Constitutionality of Democracy* (Cambridge: Cambridge University Press, 2007).

Berns, Walter, 'The Constitution as Bill of Rights' in Robert A. Goldwin and William A. Schambra (eds) *How Does the Constitution Secure Rights* (Washington, DC, and London: American Enterprise Institute for Public Policy Research, 1985) 50–73.

Besson, Samantha, 'Whose Constitution(s)? International Law, Constitutionalism and Democracy' in Jeffrey L. Dunoff and Joel P. Trachtman (eds) *Ruling the World? Constitutionalism, International Law and Global Governance* (Cambridge: Cambridge University Press, 2009) 381–408.

Bhandari, Surendra, *Global Constitutionalism and the Path of International Law. Transformation of Law and State in the Globalized World* (Leiden and Boston: Brill Nijhoff, 2016).

Bligh-Abramski, Irit, 'The Judiciary (Qādīs) as a Governmental-Administrative Tool in Early Islam' (1992) 35 *Journal of the Economic and Social History of the Orient* 40–71.

Bolingbroke, Henry St. John, *A Dissertation upon Parties In Several Letters to Caleb D'Anvers* (London: 1735, 3rd ed.).

Bourdieu, Pierre, 'Le capital social' (1980) 31 *Actes de recherché en sciences sociales* 2–3.

Bourdieu, Pierre, 'De la maison du roi a la raison d'Etat. Un modèle de la genèse du champ bureaucratique (1997) 118 *Actes de la recherché en sciences sociales* 55–68. Translated into English as 'From the King's House to the Reason of State: A Model of the Genesis of the Bureaucratic Field' (2004) 11 *Constellations* 16–36.

Bourdieu, Pierre, 'Esprits d'Etat. Genèse et structure du champ bureaucratique' (1993) 96–97 *Actes de la recherche en sciences sociales* 49–62. Translated into English as 'Rethinking the State: Genesis and Structure of the Bureaucratic Field' (1994) 12 *Sociological Theory* 1–18.

Bourdieu, Pierre, *Esquisse d'une théorie de la pratique* (Genève: Droz, 1972).

Bourdieu, Pierre, 'La force du droit [Eléments pour une sociologie du champ juridique' (1986) 64 *Actes de recherche en sciences sociales* 3–19. Translated into English as 'The Force of law. Towards a Sociology of the Juridical Field' (1987) 38 *Hastings Law Journal* 805–853.

Bourdieu, Pierre, *Langage et pouvoir symbolique* (Paris: Seuil, 2001). Translated into English as *Language and Symbolic Power* (Cambridge: Polity 1991).

Bourdieu, Pierre, *La Noblesse d'État. Grandes écoles et esprit de corps* (Paris: Les editions de minuit, 1989). Translated into English as *The State Nobility. Elite Schools in the Field of Power* (Stanford: Stanford University Press, 1996).

Bourdieu, Pierre, 'Social Space and Symbolic Power' (1989) 17 *Sociological Theory* 14–25.

Bourdieu, Pierre, *Sur l'État. Cours au Collège de France (1989–1992)* (Raison d'agir/Seuil, 2012). Translated into English as *On the State. Lectures at the Collège de France 1989–1992* (Cambridge: Polity, 2015).

Bourdieu, Pierre, and Loïc J.D. Wacquant (trans) 'Symbolic Capital and Social Classes' (2013) 13 *Journal of Classical Sociology* 292–302.

Bousquet, Georges Henri, and Schacht, Joseph, (eds) *Selected Works of C. Snouck Hurgronje* (Leiden: Brill, 1957).

ButleRitchie, David T., 'The Confines of Modern Constitutionalism' (2004–2005) 3 *Pierce Law Review* 1–32.

Carrozza, Paolo, 'Constitutionalism's Post-Modern Opening' in Martin Loughlin and Neil Walker (eds) *The Paradox of Constitutionalism: Constituent Power and Constitutional Form* (Oxford: Oxford University Press, 2007) 169–187.

Castiglione, Dario, 'The Political Theory of the Constitution' (1996) 44 *Political Studies* 417–435.

Chandler, David, (ed) *Rethinking Human Rights. Critical Approaches to International Politics* (Basingstoke and New York: Palgrave Macmillan, 2002).

Clapham, Andrew, 'The Role of the Individual in International Law' (2010) 21 *European Journal of International Law* 25–30.

Cohen, Jean L. 'Constitutionalism Beyond the State: Myth or Necessity: (A Pluralist Approach)' (2011) 2 *Humanity: An International Journal of Human Rights, Humanitarianism and Development* 127–158.

Coulson, Noel J., *Conflicts and Tensions in Islamic Jurisprudence* (Chicago, 1969).

Coulson, Noel J., *Introduction to Islamic Law* (Edinburgh: Edinburgh University Press, 1964).

Crawford, James, *Brownlie's Principles of Public International Law*, 8th edition (Oxford: Oxford University Press, 2012).

Crook, Peter J., 'Language, Truth and Law in Ancient Greece' (1985) 5 *Language and Communication* 231–263.

Dahl, Robert A., *Democracy and Its Critics* (New Haven and London: Yale University Press, 1989).

Dahl, Robert A., 'What Political Institutions Does Large Scale Democracy Require' (2005) 120 *Political Science Quarterly* 187–197.

d'Aspremont, Jean, 'International Legal Constitutionalism, Legal Forms, and the Need for Villains' (2016) Amsterdam Law School Research Paper No 2016-36, available at https://papers.ssrn.com/sol3/papers.cfm?abstract_id=2836930##.

Deleuze, Gilles, 'Bartleby or the Formula' in Gilles Deleuze, *Essays Critical and Clinical* (Minneapolis: University of Minnesota Press, 1997).

Deleuze, Gilles and Guattari, Félix, *Kafka: pour une littérature mineure* (Paris: Les éditions de minuit, 1975) Translated into English as *Kafka: Towards a Minor Literature* (Minneapolis: University of Minnesota Press, 1986).

Derrida, Jacques, *Rogues: Two Essays on Reason* (Stanford: Stanford University Press, 2004).

Derrida, Jacques, *Séminaire. La bête et le souverain* (Paris: Galilée, 2008).

De Wet, Erika, 'The Emergence of International and Regional Value Systems as a Manifestation of the Emerging International Constitutional Order' (2006) 19 *Leiden Journal of International Law* 611–632.

De Wet, Erika 'The International Constitutional Order' (2006) 55 *International and Comparative Law Quarterly* 51–76.

Dippel, Horst, 'Modern Constitutionalism, an Introduction to a History in Need of Writing' (2005) 73 *Tijdschrift voor Rechtsgeschiedenis* 153–169.

Doeser, Marinus C., and Kraay, John N. (eds) *Facts and Values. Philosophical Reflections from Western and Non-Western Perspectives* (Dordrecht/Boston/Lancaster: Martinus Nijhoff, 1986).

Douzinas, Costas, *Human Rights and Empire: The Political Philosophy of Cosmopolitanism* (Abington and New York: Routledge and Cavendish, 2007).

Doyle, Michael W., 'The UN Charter – A Global Constitution?' in Jeffrey L. Dunoff and Joel P. Trachtman (eds) *Ruling the World? Constitutionalism, International Law and Global Governance* (Cambridge: Cambridge University Press, 2009) 113–132.

Dunoff, Jeffrey L., and Trachtman, Joel P., 'A Functional Approach to International Constitutionalization' in Dunoff and Trachtman (eds) *Ruling the World? Constitutionalism, International Law and Global Governance* (Cambridge: Cambridge University Press, 2009) 3–35.

Dunoff, Jeffrey L., and Trachtman, Joel P., (eds.) *Ruling the World? Constitutionalism, International Law, and Global Governance* (Cambridge: Cambridge University Press, 2009).

Duns Scotus, John, *Quaestiones super libros metaphysicorum Aristotelis*, cum summariis, notis et scholiis RPF Hugonis Cavelli, cum annotationibus RPF Mauritii de Portu (ed de Lyon: L. Durand, 1639).

Durkheim, Emile, *Leçons de sociologie. Physique des mœurs et du droit.* (Paris: Presses universitaires de France, 1950).

Dworkin, Ronald, *Taking Rights Seriously* (Cambridge, MA: Harvard University Press, 1977).

Ehrenberg, Victor, *Aspects of the Ancient World* (Oxford: Basil Blackwell, 1946).

Ehrenberg, Victor, *Die Rechtsidee im frühen Griechentum* (Leipzig: Verlag von S. Hirzel, 1921).

Elias, Taslim Olawale, *New Horizons in International Law* (Alphen aan den Rijn: Sijthoff and Noordhoff, 1979).

Fassbender, Bardo, 'Rediscovering a Forgotten Constitution: Notes on the Place of the UN Charter in the International Legal Order' in Jeffrey L. Dunoff and Joel P. Trachtman (eds) *Ruling the World? Constitutionalism, International Law and Global Governance* (Cambridge: Cambridge University Press, 2009) 133–148.

Fassbender, Bardo, 'Sovereignty and Constitutionalism' in Neil Walker (ed.) *Sovereignty in Transition* (Oxford: Hart Publishing, 2003) 115–144.

Fassbender, Bardo, 'The United Nations Charter as Constitution of the International Community', (1998) 36 *Columbia Journal of Transnational Law* 529–619.

Fassbender, Bardo, *The United Nations Charter as the Constitution of the International Community* (Leiden, Boston: Martinus Nijhoff, 2009).

Fassbender, Bardo, '"We the People of the United Nations" Constituent Power and Constitutional Form in International Law' in Martin Loughlin and Neil Walker (eds) *The Paradox of Constitutionalism. Constituent Power and Constitutional Form* (Oxford: Oxford University Press, 2007) 269–290.

Fischer-Lescano, Andreas, 'Die Emergenz der Globalverfassung' (2003) 63 *Zeitschrift für ausländisches öffentliches Recht und Völkerrecht* 717–760.

Fischer-Lescano, Andreas, *Globalverfassung. Die Geltungsbegründung der Menschenrechte* (Weilerswist: Velbrück, 2005).

Frank, Thomas, 'Is the UN Charter a Constitution?' in Jochen A. Frowein et al. (eds) *Verhandlungen für den Frieden – Negotiating for Peace: Liber Amicorum Tono Eitel* (Berlin: Springer, 2003) 95–106.

Gagarin, Michael, 'Dike in Archaic Greek Thought' (1974) 69 *Classical Philology* 186–197.

Gagarin, Michael, 'Dikē in the Works and Days' (1973) 68 *Classical Philology* 81–94.

Gaja, Giorgio, 'The Position of Individuals in International Law: An ILC Perspective' (2010) 21 *European Journal of International Law* 11–14.

Gardbaum, Stephen, 'Human Rights and International Constitutionalism' in Jeffrey L. Dunoff and Joel R. Trachtman (eds) *Ruling the World? Constitutionalism, International Law, and Global Governance* (Cambridge: Cambridge University Press, 2009) 233–257.

Giegerich, Thomas, 'The Is and Ought of International Constitutionalism: How Far Have We Come on Habermas's Road to a "Well-Considered Constitutionalization of International Law"?' (2009) 10 *German Law Journal* 31–62.

Goitein, Shelomo D., "The Birth-Hour of Muslim Law?' (1960) 50 *Muslim World* 23.

Goldziher, Ignaz, *Vorlesungen über den Islam*, 2nd edition (Heidelberg: Carl Winter, 1925).

Griffiths, John, 'What Is Legal Pluralism?' (1986) 24 *Journal of Legal Pluralism and Unofficial Law* 2–55.

Habermas, Jürgen, 'The Crisis of the European Union in the Light of a Constitutionalization of International Law' (2012) 23 *European Journal of International Law* 335–348.

Hallaq, Wael B., 'Groundwork of the Moral Law: A New Look at the Qur'ān and the Genesis of Sharīʿa' (2009) 16 *Islamic Law and Society* 239–279.

Hallaq, Wael B., 'Ifta' and Ijtihad in Sunni Legal Theory: A Developmental Account' in Muhammad Khalid Masud, Brinkley Messick and David S. Powers (eds) *Islamic Legal Interpretation. Muftis and Their Fatwas* (Cambridge, MA: Harvard University Press, 1996) 33–43.

Hallaq, Wael B., *The Impossible State: Islam, Politics, and Modernity's Moral Predicament* (New York: Columbia University Press, 2013).

Hallaq, Wael B., 'Juristic Authority v State Power: The Legal Crises of Modern Islam' (2003) 19 *Journal of Law and Religion* 243–258.

Hallaq, Wael B., '"Muslim Rage" and Islamic Law' (2003) 54 *Hastings Law Journal* 1705–1719.

Hallaq, Wael B., *The Origins and Evolution of Islamic Law. Themes in Islamic Law* (Cambridge: Cambridge University Press, 2005).

Hallaq, Wael B., 'Qur'ānic Constitutionalism and Moral Governmentality. Further Notes on the Founding Principles of Islamic Society and Polity' (2012) 8 *Comparative Islamic Studies* 1–51.

Hallaq, Wael B., *Sharīʿa: Theory, Practice, Transformations* (Cambridge: Cambridge University Press, 2009).

Heinimann, Felix, *Nomos und Physis,: Herrkunft und Bedeutung einer Antithese im Griechischen Denken des 5. Jahrhunderts* (Stuttgart: Wissenschaftlische Buchgesellschaft, 1945).

Henkin, Louis, 'Constitutionalism and Human Rights' in Louis Henkin and Albert J. Rosenthal (eds) *Constitutionalism and Rights. The Influence of the United States Constitution Abroad* (New York: Columbia University Press, 1990) 383–395.

Holtzendorff, Franz von, *Handbuch des Völkerrechts* (Hamburg: Verlag von Carl Habel, 1877).

Johansen, Baber, *Contingency in a Sacred Law: Legal and Ethical Norms in the Muslim Fiqh* (Leiden, Boston and Köln: Brill, 1999).

Kadelbach, Stefan and Kleinlein, Thomas, 'International Law – a Constitution for Mankind? An Attempt at a Re-Appraisal with an Analysis of Constitutional Principles' (2007) 50 *German Yearbook of International Law* 303–347.

Karakulian, E.A., 'The Idea of the International Community in the History of the International Law' (2016) 1 *Jus Gentium* 581–590.

Kennedy, David, *Dark Sides of Virtue: Reassessing International Humanitarianism* (Princeton: Princeton University Press, 2004).

Kjaer, Poul F., *Constitutionalism in the Global Realm* (New York and London: Routledge, 2014).

Klabbers, Jan, Peters, Anne and Ulfstein, Geir, *The Constitutionalization of International Law* (Oxford: Oxford University Press, 2009).

Kleinlein, Thomas, 'Alfred Verdross as a Founding Father of International Constitutionalism?' (2012) 4 *Goettingen Journal of International Law* 385–416.

Kleinlein, Thomas, *Konstitutionalisierung im Völkerrecht: Konstruktion und Elemente einer idealistischen Völkerrechtslehre* (Berlin: Springer, 2011).

Krisch, Nico, *Beyond Constitutionalism: The Pluralist Structure of Postnational Law* (Oxford: Oxford University Press, 2012).

Kumin, Judith, *Welcoming Engagement. How Private Sponsorship Can Strengthen the Refugee Resettlement in the European Union* (Washington, DC: Migration Policy Institute, 2015).

Kumm, Mattias, 'The Cosmopolitan Turn in Constitutionalism: On the Relationship between Constitutionalism in and beyond the State' in Jeffrey L. Dunoff and Joel P. Trachtman (eds) *Ruling the World? Constitutionalism, International Law and Global Governance* (Cambridge: Cambridge University Press, 2009) 258–324.

Kumm, Mattias, 'The Legitimacy of International Law: A Constitutionalist Framework of Analysis' (2004) 15 *European Journal of International Law* 907–931.

Labunski, Richard, *James Madison and the Struggle for the Bill of Rights* (Oxford: Oxford University Press, 2006).

Lapidus, Ira M., 'Book Review of The Impossible State' (2015) 50 *Canadian Journal of History* 204–206.

Lapidus, Ira M., *Muslim Cities in the Later Middle Ages* (Cambridge: Cambridge University Press, 1967).

Laroche, Emmanuel, *L'Histoire de la racine NEM en grec ancient* (Paris: Librairie C. Klincksieck, 1949).

Leiter, Brian, 'Who Is the 'Sovereign Individual'? Nietzsche on Freedom' in Simon May (ed.) *Nietzsche's On the Genealogy of Morality: A Critical Guide* (Cambridge: Cambridge University Press, 2010) 101–119.

Lenzerini, Frederico, 'Sovereignty Revisited: International Law and Parallel Sovereignty of Indigenous People' (2006) 42 *Texas International Law Journal* 155–189.

Les Benedict, Michael, *The Blessings of Liberty: A Concise History of the Constitution of the United States* (Lanham: Rowman & Littlefield, 2016).

Lewis, John David, *Solon the Thinker. Political Thought in Archaic Athens*, (London: Bloomsbury, 2006).

Lindahl, Hans, 'The Paradox of Constituent Power. The Ambiguous Self-Construction of the European Union' (2007) 20 *Ratio Juris* 485–505.

Loughlin, Martin, 'Constitutional Theory: A 25th Anniversary Essay' (2005) 25 *Oxford Journal of Legal Studies* 183–202.

Loughlin, Martin, *The Foundations of Public Law* (Oxford: Oxford University Press, 2010).

Loughlin, Martin, *The Idea of Public Law* (Oxford: Oxford University Press, 2003).

Luhmann, Niklas, 'Differentiation in Society' (1977) 2 *The Canadian Journal of Sociology* 29–53.

Luhmann, Niklas, *Die Gesellschaft der Gesellschaft*, vol. 1 (Frankfurt am Main: Suhrkamp, 1997).

Luhmann, Niklas, *Grundrechte als Institution. Ein Betrag zur politischen Soziologie* (Berlin: Duncker & Humbolt, 1965).

Luhmann, Niklas, 'Individuum, Individualitaet, Individualismus' in Niklas Luhmann (ed.) *Gesellschaftstruktur und Semantik. Studien zur Wissenssoziologie der modernen Gesellschaft*, Band 3 (Frankfurt am Main: Suhrkamp, 1989) 149–258.

Luhmann, Niklas, 'Inklusion und Exklusion' in Niklas Luhmann (ed.) *Soziologische Aufklärung 6. Die Soziologie und der Mensch* (Opladen: Westdeutscher Verlag, 1995) 237–264.

Luhmann, Niklas, 'Das Paradox der Menschenrechte und drei Formen seiner Entfaltung' in Niklas Luhmann (ed.) *Soziologische Aufklärung 6. Die Soziologie und der Mensch* (Opladen: Westdeutscher Verlag, 1995) 229–236.

Luhmann, Niklas, *Politik der Gesellschaft* (Frankfurt am Main: Suhrkamp, 2000).

Luhmann, Niklas, 'Politische Verfassungen im Kontext des Gesellschaftssystems (Teil 2)' (1973) 12 *Der Staat* 165–182.

Luhmann, Niklas, *Das Recht der Gesellschaft* (Frankfurt am Main: Suhrkamp, 1993) Translated into English as *Law as a Social System* (Oxford: Oxford University Press, 2004).

Luhmann, Niklas, 'Subjektive Rechte: Zum Umbau des Rechtsbewuβtseins für die modern Gesellschaft' in Niklas Luhmann (ed.) *Gesellschaftsstruktur und Semantik. Studien zur Wissenssoziologie der modernen Gesellschaft*, Band 2, (Frankfurt am Main: Suhrkamp, 1981) 45–104.

Luhmann, Niklas, 'Die Weltgesellschaft' in Niklas Luhmann (ed.) *Soziologische Aufkläring 2. Aufsätze zur Theorie der Gesellschaft*. 4th ed. (Wiesbaden: Springer, 1991) 51–71.

Luhmann, Niklas, 'The World Society as a Social System' (1982) 8 *International Journal of General Systems* 131–138.

Macdonald, Ronald St.-J., 'The United Nations Charter: Constitution or Contract?' in Ronald St.-J. Macdonald and Douglas M. Johnston (eds) *The Structure and*

Process of International Law: Essays in Legal Philosophy, Doctrine and Theory (The Hague, Boston and Lancaster: Martinus Nijhoff, 1986) 889–912.

Madsen, Mikael Rask and Verschraegen, Gert, 'Making Human Rights Intelligible: An Introduction to a Sociology of Human Rights' in Mikael Rask Madsen and Gert Verschraegen (eds) *Making Human Rights Intelligible. Towards a Sociology of Human Rights* (Oxford: Hart, 2013) 1–24.

Mandaville, Jon, Muslim Judiciary of Damascus in the Late Mamluk Period (PhD Dissertation, Princeton University, 1969).

Mansfield, Nick, *The God Who Deconstructs Himself: Sovereignty and Subjectivity between Freud, Bataille, and Derrdia* (New York: Fordham University Press, 2010).

McIlwain, Charles Howard, *Constitutionalism: Ancient and Modern* (Ithaca: Cornell University Press, 1940).

Marks, Susan, 'State Centrism, International Law and the Anxieties of Influence' (2006) 19 *Leiden Journal of International Law* 339–347.

Masud, Muhammad Khalid, Messick, Brinkley, and Powers, David S., 'Muftis, Fatwas, and Islamic Legal Interpretation' in Muhammad Khalid Masud, Brinkley Messick and David S. Powers (eds) *Islamic Legal Interpretation. Muftis and Their Fatwas* (Cambridge, MA: Harvard University Press, 1996) 3–32.

Meier, Christian, 'Der Wandel der politisch-sozialen Begriffswelt im 5. Jahrhundert v. Chr.' (1977) 21 *Archiv für Begriffsgeschichte* 7–41.

Meiksins Wood, Ellen, *Citizens to Lords: A Social History of Western Political Thought from Antiquity to the Late Middle Ages* (London and New York: Verso, 2008).

Merry, Sally Engle, 'Legal Pluralism' (1988) 22 *Law and Society Review* 869–896.

Michaels, Ralf, 'The Functional Method of Comparative Law' in Mathias Reimann and Reinhard Zimmermann (eds) *The Oxford Handbook of Comparative Law* (Oxford: Oxford University Press, 2006) 339–382.

Morgan, Robert J., *James Madison on the Constitution and the Bill of Rights* (Westport, CT: Greenwood Press, 1988).

Motzki, Harald, *The Origins of Islamic Jurisprudence: Meccan Fiqh before the Classical Schools* (Leiden and Boston: Brill, 2002).

Nardo, Don, (ed.) *The Creation of the US Constitution* (San Diego: Greenhaven Press, 2005).

Negri, Antonio, *Insurgencies: Constituent Power and the Modern State* (Minneapolis: University of Minnesota Press, 1999).

O'Donoghue, Aoife, 'Alfred Verdross and the Contemporary Constitutionalization Debate' (2012) 32 *Oxford Journal of Legal Studies* 799–822.

O'Donoghue, Aoife, *Constitutionalism in Global Constitutionalisation* (Cambridge: Cambridge University Press, 2014).

O'Donoghue, Aoife, 'International Constitutionalism and the State' (2013) 11 *International Journal of Constitutional Law* 1021–1045.

Ostwald, Martin, *From Popular Sovereignty to the Sovereignty of Law. Law, Society, and Politics in Fifth-Century Athens* (Berkley and Los Angeles: University of California Press, 1986).

Ostwald, Martin, *Nomos and the Beginnings of Athenian Democracy* (Oxford: Clarendon Press, 1969).

Ostwald, Martin, 'Pindar, Nomos and Heracles: (Pindar, Frg. 169 [Snell2]+POxy. No. 2450, Frg. I): Dedicated to Harry Caplan' (1965) 69 *Harvard Studies in Classical Philology* 109–138.

Owens, Ron, *Solon of Athens: Poet, Philosopher, Soldier, Statesman* (Brighton: Sussex Academic Press, 2010).

Parlett, Kate, *The Individual in the International Legal System: Continuity and Change in International Law* (Cambridge: Cambridge University Press, 2010).

Parsons, Talcott, 'Full Citizenship for the American Negro? A Sociological Problem' (1965) 94 *Daedelus* 1009–1054.

Parsons, Talcott, *Societies: Evolutionary and Comparative Perspectives* (Englewood Cliffs: Prentice Hall, 1966).

Patton, Walter M., *Ahmed Ibn Hanbal and the Mihna. A Contribution to a Biography of the Imâm and to the History of the Mohammedan Inquisition Called the Mihna, 218–234 A. H.* (Leiden: Brill, 1897).

Paulus, Andreas L., 'The International Legal System as a Constitution' in Jeffrey L. Dunoff and Joel R. Trachtman (eds.) *Ruling the World? Constitutionalism, International Law, and Global Governance* (Cambridge: Cambridge University Press, 2009) 69–111.

Peters, Anne, 'Are We Moving Towards Constitutionalization of the World Community?' in Antonio Cassese (ed.) *Realizing Utopia: The Future of International Law* (Oxford: Oxford University Press, 2012) 118–135.

Peters, Anne, 'Dual Democracy' in Jan Klabbers, Anne Peters, and Geir Ulfstein (eds.) *The Constitutionalization of International Law* (Oxford: Oxford University Press, 2009) 263–341.

Peters, Anne, *Jenseits der Menschenrechte. Die Rechtsstellung des Individuums im Völkerrecht* (Tübingen: Mohr Siebeck, 2014) translated as *Beyond Human Rights: The Legal Status of the Individual in International Law* (Cambridge: Cambridge University Press, 2016).

Petersen, Niels, 'Die Wandel des ungeschriebenen Völkerrechts im Zuge der Konstitutionalisierung' (2008) 46 *Archiv des Völkerrechts* 502–523.

Petersmann, Ernst-Ulrich, 'How to Constitutionalize International Law and Foreign Policy for the Benefit of Civil Society?' (1998) 20 *Michigan Journal of International Law* 1–30.

Petersmann, Ernst-Ulrich, 'Human Rights and the Law of the World Trade Organization.' (2003) 37 *Journal of World Trade* 241–281.

Petersmann, Ernst-Ulrich, 'Time for a United Nations 'Global Compact' for Integrating Human Rights into the Law of Worldwide Organizations: Lessons from European Integration' (2002) 13 *European Journal of International Law* 621–650.

Pokorny, Julius, *Indogermanisches Etymologisches Wörterbuch* (Bern, München: Francke Verlag, 1959).

Powers, David S., 'Legal Consultation (futyā) in Medieval Spain and North Africa' in Mallat Chibli (ed.) *Islam and Public Law: Classical and Contemporary Studies* (London and Boston: Graham and Trotman, 1993) 85–106.

Raaflaub, Kurt A., 'Early Greek Political Thought in Its Mediterranean Context' in Ryan K. Balot (ed.) *A Companion to Greek and Roman Political Thought* (Malden, MA: Wiley-Blackwell, 2009) 37–56.

Rancière, Jacques, *Disagreement: Politics and Philosophy* (Minneapolis: The University of Minnesota Press, 1999).

Randall, Bernard, *Solon: The Lawmaker of Athens* (New York: Rosen Publishing, 2004).

Remec, Peter P., *The Position of the Individual in International Law According to Grotius and Vattel* (The Hague: Martinus Nijjhof, 1960).

Rolland, Jean-Claude, *Les grandes familles des mots* (Raleigh: Lulu Editions, 2011).

Rosen, Lawrence, *The Anthropology of Justice: Law as Culture in Islamic Society* (Cambridge: Cambridge University Press, 1989).

Rosenfeld, Michael, *The Identity of the Constitutional Subject* (London and New York: Routledge, 2010).

Rosenfeld, Michael, 'Modern Constitutionalism as Interplay between Identity and Diversity: An Introduction' (1992–1993) 14 *Cardozo Law Review* 497–532.

Rutland, Robert A., *The Birth of the Bill of Rights, 1776-1791* (Chapel Hill: University of North Carolina Press, 1955).

Rutland, Robert A., 'How the Constitution Protects Our Rights: A Look at the Seminal Years' in Robert A. Goldwin and William A. Schambra (eds) *How Does the Constitution Secure Rights* (Washington, DC, and London: American Enterprise Institute for Public Policy Research, 1985), 1–14.

Schacht, Joseph, *Introduction to Islamic Law* (Oxford: Oxford University Press, 1982).

Schmitt, Carl, *Der Begriff des Politischen.* Text von 1932 mit einem Vorwort und drei Corollarien (Berlin: Duncker & Humbolt, 1963) Translated into English as *The Concept of the Political* (Chicago and London: University of Chicago Press, 1996).

Schmitt, Carl, *The Nomos of the Earth in the International Law of the Jus Publicum Europaeum* (New York: Telos Press, 2003).

Schwöbel, Christine, *Global Constitutionalism in International Legal Perspective* (Leiden and Boston: Martinus Nijhoff, 2011).

Sciulli, David, *Theory of Societal Constitutionalism. Foundations of a Non-Marxist Critical Theory* (Cambridge: Cambridge University Press, 1992).

Scott, Paul, '(Political) Constitutions and (Political) Constitutionalism' (2013) 4 *German Law Journal* 2157–2184.

Segal, Schulim, *L'individu en droit international positif* (Paris: Recueil Sirey, 1932).

Shaw, Malcolm N., *Public International Law*, 7th edition (Cambridge: Cambridge University Press, 2014).

Simma, Bruno and Paulus, Andreas L., 'The "International Community": Facing the Challenge of Globalisation' (1998) 9 *European Journal of International Law* 266–277.

Smend, Rudolf, 'Verfassung and Verfassungsrecht' in Rudolf Smend (ed.) *Staatsrechtliche Abhandlungen* (Berlin: Duncker and Humblot, 1965) 199–277.

Somek, Alexander, *The Cosmopolitan Constitution* (Oxford: Oxford University Press, 2014).

Spiropoulos, Johannes, 'L'individu et le droit international' (1929) 30 *Hague Academy of International Law. Recueil des cours V* 191–270.

Stratton, Jon, 'Writing and Law in Ancient Greece' (1980) 14 *Visible Language* 99–120.

Teubner, Gunter, *Constitutional Fragments: Societal Constitutionalism and Globalisation* (Oxford: Oxford University Press, 2012).

Teubner, Gunter, 'Global Bukowina: Legal Pluralism in the World Society', in Gunter Teubner (ed.) *Global Law without a State* (Aldershot: Dartmouth, 1997) 3–28.

Teubner, Gunter, 'Societal Constitutionalism: Alternatives to State-Centred Constitutional Theory?' in Christian Joerges, Inge-Johanne Sand and Gunter Teubner (eds) *Constitutionalism and Transnational Governance* (Oxford: Hart Publishing, 2004) 3–28.

Thornhill, Chris, 'Niklas Luhmann and the Sociology of the Constitution' (2010) 10 *Journal of Classical Sociology* 315–337.

Thornhill, Chris, 'Rights and Constituent Power in the Global Constitution' (2014) 10 *International Journal of Law in Context* 357–396.

Thornhill, Chris, *A Sociology of Constitutions. Constitutions and State Legitimacy in Historical-Sociological Perspective* (Cambridge: Cambridge University Press, 2011).

Thornhill, Chris, *A Sociology of Transnational Constitutions. Social Foundations of the Post-National Legal Structure* (Cambridge: Cambridge University Press, 2016).

Thornhill, Chris, 'State Building, Constitutional Rights and the Social Construction of Norms: Outline for a Sociology of Constitutions' in Mikael

Rask Madsen and Gert Verschraegen (eds) *Making Human Rights Intelligible. Towards a Sociology of Human Rights* (Oxford: Hart, 2013) 25–60.

Tornaritis, Criton G., *The Individual as a Subject of International Law* (Nicosia: Public Information Office, 1972).

Van Mulligen, Johannes Gerald, 'Global Constitutionalism and the Objective Purport of the International Legal Order' (2011) 24 *Leiden Journal of International Law* 277–304.

Vec, Miloš, 'From the Congress of Vienna to the Paris Peace Treaties of 1919' in Bardo Fassbender and Anne Peters (eds) *The Oxford Handbook of the History of International Law* (Oxford: Oxford University Press, 2012) 654–678.

Verdross, Alfred, *Einheit des rechtlichen Weltbildes auf Grundlage der Völkerrechtsverfassung* (Tübingen: JCB Mohr Siebeck, 1923).

Verdross, Alfred, *Die Verfassung des Völkerrechtsgemeinschaft* (Wien and Berlin: Springer, 1926).

Verschraegen, Gert, 'Differentiation and Inclusion: A Neglected Sociological Approach to Fundamental Rights' in Mikael Rask Madsen and Gert Verschraegen (eds) *Making Human Rights Intelligible. Towards a Sociology of Human Rights* (Oxford: Hart, 2013) 61–80.

Vlastos, Gregory, 'Isonomia' (1953) 74 *The American Journal of Philology* 337–366.

Walker, Neil, 'Constitutionalism and Pluralism in Global Context' in M. Avbelj and J. Komarek (eds) *Constitutional Pluralism in the European Union and Beyond.* Studies of the Oxford Institute of European & Comparative Law (Oxford: Hart, 2012) 17–38.

Walker, Neil, 'Postnational Constitutionalism and Postnational Public Law: A Tale of Two Neologisms', (2012) 3 *Transnational Legal Theory* 61–85.

Weber, Max, 'Politik als Beruf' in Max Weber, *Gesammelte Politische Schriften* (München: Drei Masken Verlag, 1921) 396–450.

Weiss, Bernard G., *The Spirit of Islamic Law* (Athens and London: The University of Georgia Press, 1968).

Werner, Wouter, 'The Never-Ending Closure: Constitutionalism and International Law' in Nicholas Tsagourias (ed.) *Transnational Constitutionalism: International and European Perspectives* (Cambridge: Cambridge University Press, 2010) 329–367.

Wheatley, Steven, *The Democratic Legitimacy of International Law* (Oxford and Portland: Hart, 2010).

Wielke, Janina, *Die Mihna im Kontext abbasidischer Machtpolitik* (Norderstedt: GRIN, 2011).

Wiener, Antje et al., 'Global Constitutionalism: Human Rights, Democracy, and the Rule of Law' (2012) 1 *Global Constitutionalism* 1–15.

Wormuth, Francis D., *The Origins of Modern Constitutionalism* (New York: Harper & Brothers, 1949).

Yahyaoui Krivenko, Ekaterina, 'Hospitality and Sovereignty: What Can We Learn from the Canadian Private Sponsorship of Refugees Programme' (2012) 24 *International Journal of Refugee Law* 579–602.

Yahyaoui Krivenko, Ekaterina, 'International Law, Literature and Interdisciplinarity' (2015) 9 *Law and Humanities* 103–122.

Yahyaoui Krivenko, Ekaterina, *Women, Islam and International Law within the Context of the Convention on the Elimination of All Forms of Discrimination against Women* (Leiden, Boston: Brill, 2009).

Yoshida, Kei, *Rationality and Cultural Interpretivism. A Critical Assessment of Failed Solutions* (Lanham: Lexington Books, 2014).

Zaman, Muhammad Qasim, 'The Caliphs, the "Ulamā", and the Law: Defining the Role and Functions of the Caliph in Early 'Abbāsid Period' (1997) 4 *Islamic Law and Society* 1–36.

INDEX